A "Justice 4 Every1" book production series. Profits from this book will go to assisting elders and disableds fight for their civil and human rights in probate courts across this nation.

Email us at: Joanne@Justice4every1.com and see our website at www.justice4every1.com.

You may email Teresa Lyles at: tozzolyles@gmail.com.

1st Edition November 16, 2016

<u>Cover Artwork</u> – the cover art work was a pencil drawing by Julio Hernandez-Rojo, my cousin, and my mom's nephew. The artwork was given to me, and other family members, as a Christmas present in December 1990. Julio passed away in 1994.

65 MINUTES[1]

A Tale of Torture and Murder in Guardianship

By Teresa Tozzo-Lyles

---

[1]This is the amount of time it took a panel of three to declare Ms. Carmen Tozzo incompetent.

CHAPTER ONE

The End and The Beginning

The afternoon before my mom went to heaven, I lay in bed with her - she was weak from the massive doses of highly toxic and lethal drugs they had been giving her. She was bruised, she could not move, she did not want to be touched, and she even refused to drink her Cuban coffee, her "café-cito."

I had gotten into bed with her because she could not go anywhere else. As we both held hands, her head on my shoulder, I listened to her steady, rhythmic breathing. I closed my eyes and felt a sense of peace that had eluded me for almost four years since the guardianship nightmare began. I did not realize it then, but my angel was giving me an indication of how it would be for her when she left this earth – total peace, comfort, and love.

My mom suffered and was in horrible pain at the end of her life – the guardian, hospice, and my sisters made sure of that. The effects of the drugs, and the injury to her right foot (swollen ankle and pressure wound on her heel), was excruciating even at the lightest touch. As I watched her go through this, I felt helpless, angry, bitter, and afraid as I had so many times before. I was threatened with arrest, even during the last week of my mom's life. My mom NEVER complained and she refused to be a victim. She KNEW what was happening despite the abuse, the neglect and the drugs. She ALWAYS KNEW.

My story is perhaps no different than thousands of those that came before me, and those still fighting to see, and free, their loved ones from guardianship. However, my case was not only about taking her money, but about trying to "eliminate" my mom and separating her from everything she loved, including me. It was intentional.

I met with the first plenary guardian for the first time on Thursday, November 17, 2011. In an email to the guardian on

November 18, 2011, I asked for her to reconsider putting my mom in a facility, and that I would pay for all her care. She refused.

My mom's suffering under guardianship was never about what was "in her best interest," it was about money and revenge. I knew deep in my heart that this first guardian was going to do what my sisters wanted, which was to remove my mom from her home, separate her from the family members who cared about her the most, and try to cause as much emotional and financial damage to me as possible. What I didn't know is that they wanted to dispose of her in the cruelest way, so that they could take the money they felt was rightfully theirs. I always suspected, as I had with anything done under probate, that all three guardians and my sisters were siphoning money out under the color of the law.

I knew the first guardian was involved in every aspect of my mother's demise and her lack of care, even after she resigned, but I could not prove it. That is, until after my mom died when I saw the accounting submitted to the courts in December 2015, so that the first and third guardians, and their attorney, could drain the remaining amount from my mom's bank account. I was never allowed to see what the guardians submitted to the courts as expenses for my mom's care. My mom also did not know what they were spending and on what. The amounts did not add up.

On May 24, 2015, my bright light shone no more. The pain of losing her has not eased with time, it has only worsened. Every time I feel angry and resentful, I think about her smile, her kindness, her touch, her kisses, and most importantly her words to me, "pray, and leave it in God's hands, that is all you can do." I want to honor my mom with being in peace, serenity, joy, and continuing the love of family and God she always cherished.

How did this tragedy ever happen in my family?

I thought our family was so full of love, compassion, and caring. We were a traditional family that was so full of respect for grandparents, parents and children. The answer is guardianship, which is generally an area of the court system that operates directly under probate court. And of course as it pertained to my family, as the saying goes, "one (or two) bad apples will spoil the bunch."

Guardianship is a form of modern day slavery, except that slaves of past always had hope that they would one day be set free. Wards of the state have no identity, no rights, and no property. They cannot marry, vote, defend themselves, control their environment, or enter into contracts, as in my mom's case. They are not allowed to spend a single cent of their own money, or write a single check for their personal needs. They are not allowed to travel.

Historically, guardianship was established to help those who did not have family or the financial means to be cared for. However, it has turned in a multi-billion dollar exploitative business. All the wealth for every generation will pass through the nation's probate courts.

With guardians, the attorneys and probate judges, taking everything is not good enough. They also lie, cheat, defame, false light, slander and libel anyone who gets in their way of taking the money and protecting the vulnerable family member. They are even known to work with police and create set ups for false arrest of a felony, because felons cannot serve as guardians. This why they continuously threatened to have me arrested multiple times. They are like the walking dead, with no end in sight. Their evil missions will not end until they completely devour the money and assets of the victim and victim's family.

You get the picture.

CHAPTER 2
Reflections of Childhood
The Chubby Little Girl Who Climbed Trees

The first eight years of my life were spent in the small town of Hawthorne, New Jersey. I was born at St. Joseph's Hospital in Paterson. Hawthorne was a suburb consisting mostly of Italian and Irish families. Most of my friends had five or more siblings. I had two sisters. I was the middle daughter.

I grew up with my Italian family, which consisted of my dad and his two siblings – my Uncle Frank (Florestano) and Aunt Sandy "Tini" (Santina) – my grandmother Susan (Asunta), Sandy's husband, my Uncle Lou, their son, Donald, and a slew of other aunts and uncles named Joe, Tony, Lina, Jennie and others that I cannot remember, but they always stopped by for large Italian meals. We had sausage and meatballs, pasta, lasagna, manicotti, salad, wine, and fresh fruit.

My Uncle Frank married my aunt Blanca (my mom's sister). As children, we had trouble saying Uncle Frank, so we called him Unky, and for my aunt Blanca, Tia Blankita, we called her Taty.

I heard the story from both my parents about how my aunt and uncle met. When my mom and dad came back from their wedding and honeymoon to live in Hawthorne, they showed the movie of their wedding to my grandmother, aunt, and uncle. My uncle saw my aunt, a gorgeous little blond spitfire and asked "who is that!!!" My uncle, a classical violinist, wooed my aunt, and they were married about one and a half years after my mom and dad's wedding. They never had children. They were also my godparents. I was very close to both of them. I always said that I grew up with two sets of parents, because my aunt and uncle were truly like a second mother and father to me. They were amazing, and like my mom and dad, they shared a deep and passionate love. Both couples – one Cuban, one Italian – married when they were well into their 30s and early 40s. We grew up with my Unky and Taty. They lived with us in New

Jersey, and then next door to us in Miami, and also in Gainesville. We were never separated, until their deaths.

My dad and uncle were brothers and best friends, and so were my mom and aunt – sisters and best friends. The fondest memories of growing up were listening to them talk about anything and everything. These four amazing people, their sense of caring and family taught me so many lessons about love. They are a big part of my story.

I always had a sense of love, belonging, and family both in Hawthorne and Miami. I learned from both Italian and Cuban families that you respected your parents and your elders. Your elders stayed in your home until their death and were cared for by the younger generations – children, grandchildren, cousins, and other family. I had no idea what a nursing home was or what it was for until way into my adult years. I never understood why people were so cruel and put their mom or dad in such horrible facilities. They always smelled like urine and death to me. There was so much love and understanding among my family, who would ever want to put them in such a horrible place.

I had a lot to learn.

From observing, listening and feeling this amazing sense of connectedness as a child, adolescent, teenager, and young adult, I always knew that I would take care of my parents, and aunt and uncle, as they had taken care of their own families their entire lives.

I always remember being sick as a young child growing up in New Jersey. I was a fat little chubby kid with short hair and a carefree attitude. I would talk with and play with anyone. I never remember being sad in New Jersey, except when we left.

I did all the things an active little girl did. Much to my mom's chagrin, I was always climbing trees, getting dirty, having scraped and bloody knees, and catching bugs. Fireflies were my favorite. Small critters fascinated me. All animals fascinated me. My poor mom, I always ruined my beautiful Sunday dresses and pretty little frilly socks. I didn't realize it at the time, but I was just like her and my dad when they were young.

The first time I can remember being in the hospital was at about age two, then at age five, and finally about age seven. I would get the flu, could not stop vomiting, get severely dehydrated, and was then hospitalized for a couple days with IV fluids. My first memory in the hospital was lying in a crib, with restraints on my hands and legs so I wouldn't jump out, and seeing my mom and dad walking away from the room. I yelled for my mom and dad. I could tell that my mom was crying, but she did not turn around. My parents decided that the cold weather in New Jersey was not healthy for me. They decided to move to Miami, Florida, a place where our family spent two weeks of vacation each summer. We moved to Miami in 1967.

Discipline in my family was very old-school. We got spankings from my mom, dad, grandmother, aunts, and uncles. Raising children was a family responsibility. Jokingly, I always said that my dad took "the belt" to me twice, only because I did not learn my lesson the first time. With that being said, I had two of the most loving and dedicated parents in the world. They were very "hands on" with their children. Everything they had was solely to help their children and grandchildren. When the grandchildren came into the picture, I asked my parents why they didn't travel more. My dad's answer was, "why? We have our grandchildren now." They always wanted to be around their family.

My mom was a stay at home mom in New Jersey and then for a while in Miami. Since my aunt did not work either, we were around them all the time. We learned how to speak Spanish before we learned proper English. My mom did not drive, so we walked everywhere as children. And we had to walk, because my mom wasn't about to carry three little girls to the grocery store, church, or the park. I always remember my mom's smile, her love, and her devotion to God. She made us pray and say the rosary all the time. Somehow, even though I was a little girl and I wanted to go outside and play, I didn't mind doing what my mom asked. I remember never wanting to disappoint her or my dad, but mostly I never wanted to disappoint her.

My parents made the decision to move to Florida. I think part of it was because of my health issues and getting sick so much, but I also think because my mom was so homesick for her family and friends. Plus, she hated the cold weather and the snow. My dad accommodated her. He always wanted to make her happy.

I was sad to be away from my grandma, aunt and other family that I barely got to know. I was just a kid after all, but those early years were a foundation of how I would want my own family to be. My grandmother, the only grandparent that I grew up with, was such a great soul. We visited often before my grandma got sick after I was married, but before that, my aunt, uncle and grandma came down to Miami a few times to visit us. I did not know what lay ahead and what adventures would come from the move to Florida, but I know I was excited for the change. I loved the beach, just like my mom. I could not get enough of the gorgeous ocean and salt water spraying on my face when we went for our annual vacations from New Jersey to Miami Beach. I don't think my siblings were ever as excited as I was to be in the ocean.

There were only two sad memories that I had from New Jersey, both times when I was in the first grade at St. Anthony's Catholic school. We had a Monsignor, whom my mom loved and our family was very close to. He died suddenly. I don't remember him being that old. They told us at school that we had to go to the church service for him inside the church. His body was in an open casket at the front of the church.

I had never seen a dead body before, and it scared me. I had nightmares for a long time. My mom comforted me and told me it was going to be ok, she dried my tears when I cried and was scared.

She sang to me, and I would fall asleep in her arms. I loved those comforting arms.

The other sad memory involved a little boy in my class. I can't remember his name, but I remember he was Hispanic. His dad was in Vietnam, and he came home for good this time to be with his son and family. His dad came into our class with him. This little boy had a smile from ear to ear. I don't think a week had gone by after his dad had returned from Vietnam. He had stopped to help a man having car trouble on the side of the road. A drunk driver hit him, and he died instantly. I remember my dad being incredibly sad and commenting about it. He showed me the picture of the soldier who had come home to his little boy, only to die. I didn't understand much about death, but I knew from these two incidences that it wasn't fair.

Again, I had a lot to learn.

From as far as I can remember, growing up in Hawthorne, and being visited by our Cuban family, vacationing in Miami Beach, then actually living in Miami, everyone in our family that knew my mom from Cuba always said, "you are exactly like your mother." As a young child, I thought that this was only about the looks. I was blessed with a head of thick, black hair just like my mom. I was also blessed with green eyes – one paternal uncle and one maternal uncle both had green eyes. But as I grew into my own sense of self as a teenager, a young adult, a wife, and a mother, I understood more of what everyone meant.

My mom and I had this connection that was incredibly powerful. Perhaps it was my perception of our relationship, but I cannot think of anyone who had this sense of connection with their mother. Not this deep, not this intense, not this spiritual. We knew what the other was thinking, and after I left my home in Miami for college, usually when I thought about my mom, I would receive a phone call from her within minutes. After she was handed over into guardianship, and she would suffer falls and injuries, I would feel physical pain. Many times, and for years, I did not understand why my body would react and feel what it was feeling. I couldn't explain it.

After she died, I was going through some of her old pictures from Cuba. I chose one that I had seen dozens of times, but never really paid much attention to it – a picture of her when she was about age 12, on a beach in Cuba. When I scanned the picture of my mom as a young girl and enlarged it, I saw myself. It was like watching a reflection in a mirror, the same hair, and the same facial expression.

I was really was her "mini me."

Nuestra Familia/Nostra Famiglia - It Started with the Grandparents

I only knew two of my grandparents. My maternal grandmother, Ines, died a few years before my parents married, and my paternal grandfather, John (Giovanni) Tozzo moved to California after him and my grandmother, Susan, were divorced in the late 1930s. My dad was still in high school when they got divorced. That must have been so difficult for him to deal with. I always wondered if that is the reason he volunteered for the Navy. It is my understanding that divorce in those days was a HUGE ordeal, especially in Catholic Italian families. The women were stigmatized and considered to be loose and "easy." All I know about their divorce was what my grandmother told me. She said that my grandfather was cheating and having an affair with another woman. She told me that my uncle Frank had seen them in a compromising position, and told my grandmother. My grandmother did not want to divorce her husband, but my uncle, who resembled his father the most, encouraged my grandmother to proceed with the divorce. The only other thing my grandmother said about him was that he did not want any more children. She wanted a bunch. He refused to sleep in the same bed with her after my father was born.

I wish I had met my Abuela Ines. My mom and aunt always told me that she was "a saint," as did other family members. She was good, kind, loving and caring to everyone in her family. My mom, the baby of the family, was very close to her mom. My abuela died when she was only about 68 years old from, I believe, cervical cancer. I know hearing about her illness from both my mom and aunt that it took several years for her to die after the initial diagnosis. She died at home, in her bed, peacefully, surrounded by her children, grandchildren and extended family. Her family bathed and prepared her body after her death. My mom was devastated when she died. Every time she would talk about her own mother, my mom would cry. I have a few pictures of my abuela and mom when they both were young. I know that she met my abuelo, Manuel, when they were both very young, late teens, and they were married shortly after they met. I believe my mom said that my grandmother was 17 when she met my grandfather, and he was only 19. She raised eight children, with one dying in early childhood.

I grew up with my grandma Susan in New Jersey. She had a great impact on my life. She was very carefree. She was a gorgeous woman. She was also very strong, extremely intelligent, vivacious, flirty, and boy could she cook!!! She loved her family. My dad was her youngest and she always called him, "her baby." For as far back as I can remember, my mom, dad and sisters and I would go to church every Sunday, and then we would have a huge meal with my grandma, Aunt Sandy and Uncle Lou. My grandmother had an arranged marriage with my grandfather. He was in his early 30s, but she just a young teenager, probably 15. I know that she had all three of her children by the time she was 21 years old.

I know that there was some tension between my mom and grandmother and Aunt Sandy, and also between my Aunt Blanca, Aunt Sandy and my grandmother. I know that all families have issues and I think that it was mostly about who was the dominant female in the group. These were four very headstrong and stubborn women. I loved them all equally. I could never take sides.

I remember sitting in the kitchen with my grandmother for hours watching her cook. She always "talked" with her hands. She rarely had a recipe, it was all about how it tasted and if there was enough wine in her reach. My grandma was one of the oldest siblings in her family of 9 children, the Natale's. When she passed at 91, I remember thinking how much I missed seeing her between leaving New Jersey at age 8, and the time of her death. I swore that my kids would always know and visit their grandparents. She always laughed and smelled like violets.

After her stroke, she wasn't the same, she was a different person, but I guess an illness and disability does have an effect on a person. She met two of my three children before she passed. When we moved to Miami, it broke my grandmother's heart. I don't think she ever got over it. She had a stroke at age 79, and lived another 11 years, being lovingly cared for by my Aunt Sandy, her only daughter. She depended on my aunt for everything, and it was very hard on my aunt being alone as her sole caretaker. I know my dad and uncle visited when they could, and they provided some respite, but she was the one who took care of her mother full time. She refused to put her in a nursing home, even after her own husband died. I admired and loved my aunt for that. She was also a very headstrong and independent woman. She walked everywhere in her home town, because just like my mom and aunt, she never drove. She went on excursions to Atlantic City with her friends.

For me, I always remember the grandma that played "Ring Around the Rosie" and told me stories about the past, always called me "sweetie pie," and made her Italian comments like, "he's dead to me" or "all men are bums." You just can't make things like that up. She never judged and always loved. I felt bad that I didn't spend more time with her during my visits after the stroke. I was young and stupid, and probably a little selfish. I never stopped loving her. I went to her funeral in 1989.

Many years after my grandmother passed away, my Aunt Sandy, who had lived in the same two-story home in Hawthorne for more than 60 years, where she had raised her child, and taken care of my grandmother until her death, was driven to an assisted living facility. My aunt did not want to go. She was incredibly healthy and independent, but she had been having some memory problems, just like my mom had been having for a few years prior to guardianship. But honestly, most men and women in their 80s and 90s have some type of memory problem. It does NOT mean they need to be taken away from their homes, their friends, their church, and their community. There are other solutions. The solution would have been an easy fix to keeping my aunt out of the assisted living facility. My uncle and I were completely against this move, but the decision was entirely up to my aunt's only child. I loved my cousin and his wife, but I wholeheartedly disagreed with what they were doing to my aunt. I found it odd that the woman who had given life to her son and raised him, then put her life on hold and had taken care of her own mother for 11 years, was not given the same respect and dignity. I was angry and upset because my aunt had dedicated so many years of her life taking care of her own mother. She deserved better, and it seemed wrong and such a betrayal to move her away from everything she knew and loved. I felt that my cousin and his wife had the means, the room, and the wherewithal to care of my aunt.

However, another family member was in agreement with my aunt moving to the assisted living facility – my older sister. I should have known something was amiss at that time. She would be instrumental in putting my mom into a horrific guardianship against her will and mine.

A few years after my aunt was placed into an assisted living facility, and more than likely drugged, her daughter in law suffered a massive stroke. She was permanently disabled. She was fairly young, maybe about 68 or 69 years old. The freedom to travel and live a carefree lifestyle that her and her husband had desired, was taken away. My cousin has been the caregiver for his wife for many years now.

My Aunt Sandy died in 2014 at the age of 97. My aunt died alone in her room at the AL, without family. Her son told me they had brought in her evening dinner tray, and when they came back about 20 minutes later, she had passed. That she was alone in the facility saddened me more than her passing. I was not told about her passing for many months, which was intentional.

I remember my last conversation with my aunt, and it was a sad one. I remember telling my mom about her death, and she seemed sad as well, but then my mom told me that at least my aunt was now at peace. She knew my aunt was placed in the Assisted Living Facility years earlier. My mom knew she didn't deserve to be there either. My mom had already been placed under guardianship.

The few times that I spoke to my Aunt Sandy after her move to the Assisted Living Facility, she wanted to go home. She cried long and hard about how sad and miserable she felt there. She told me that she "wanted to die" if she couldn't go back to her home. She asked me to intercede and call her son. I told her I would try, but as mentioned earlier, the decision to place her there and keep her there was not one I was entitled to make. I will regret until the day I die that I only spoke to her one more time after that day. I tried several other times to call, but she was asleep or having a meal, or so they said. By that time, I was already in the middle of getting a divorce, and going through grad school. This was no excuse, by any means, but the pain of listening to my aunt sob broke my heart. I was thousands of miles away, and if her own brother, my uncle, could not change his nephew's mind, there was nothing I could have done.

But I did stay in contact with her grandchildren, and called several times asking about my aunt and their mom, after the stroke. I knew they had moved my aunt to another facility several years before she died due to the decline in her mental capacity. It was too hard for me to understand why someone would do this. I loved her dearly. I never knew that anything could be more heartbreaking than this. After my aunt's Sandy's passing, I had the opportunity to speak with her son, my cousin, for a very long time. It was heartbreaking to hear about his wife, her condition, and how my aunt had died. He had suffered a lot as well.

I learned about guardianship in 2011, the hard way.

My dad, uncle, and aunt did not die alone. They had someone in the room or in the bed holding them when they left this earth. My mom died in a small bed in the Assisted Living Facility where she resided. She died as I was walking into the facility for the last time.

From Pasta to Arroz con Pollo

I was just one year old. This was my earliest memory…of being in Cuba.

I can remember that day, those brief moments. I was sitting on my mother's lap, clapping my hands. My Aunt Julia, had handed me a tiny gray and white kitten. It was very young, and its eyes were barely open. My aunt had put a tiny pink bonnet on the kitten. I remember laughing with glee. My parents and older sister (then 3) had traveled to Cuba to visit my mom's family. We visited the farm where my mom's oldest brother, Angel, his wife Julia, and two sons were living. They always had animals, and I always had a love for any animal. My mom and I shared the love of one particular animal – horses.

Years later when I saw my Aunt Julia again in Miami for the first time since that day in Cuba, I described my memory of the kitten to her. She was shocked and surprised at the details of my memory about the little kitten. My earliest and fondest memories always included my mom and dad.

My Cuban family brought so much joy and happiness in my life, very similar to what my Italian family gave me. I had the opportunity to meet my grandfather (abuelo) Manuel when I went to Cuba as a one year old. He died when he was about 82 years old in Cuba. My mom and aunt could not go to his funeral. I was only about 5 years old when my mom got the news of his death. I remember she cried for a very long time, for many hours. I cried with her because I was sad just watching her cry. It must have been difficult for my mom and aunt to not attend the funeral of their own father whom they loved dearly. I remember stories about my grandfather, and how he was always so serious and such a disciplinarian. I guess that comes with

being the chief of police in Havana for so many years. My mom did say that when my Abuelo met me, he spoiled me and gave me what I wanted. My Tio Angel sat on the floor and played with me.

My mom and aunt always described Cuba as paradise. To them, that was what this once beautiful island represented – love, peace, innocence, friendship, education, community and family.

There were eight children in my mom's family. One child had

died at a very young age. Four girls, three boys survived – Louisa, Angel, Louis, Ines, Carlos, Blanca and Maria del Carmen (my mom). My Aunt Louisa and Uncle Angel were educated in the U.S. (New York). They both received their bachelor's degrees in education. I know that my Uncle Louis was a journalist and managed a local radio station. My aunt (Taty) worked in a lawyer's office as a legal assistant, and my mom was an

executive secretary at Parke Davis & Company (pharmaceuticals) in Havana in the late 1930s, 1940s and 1950s, until she met and married

my dad. My mom was very knowledgeable about many drugs and their interactions. This is one of the reasons she kept trying to spit out, and refused to take, the medications they kept trying to give her at the lock down facilities.

My mom was the baby of the family, and so was my dad. I only met my abuelo, and some of my aunts and uncles during this trip to Cuba. Shortly thereafter, the Revolution began, and no one could get in or out of Cuba for almost two decades. Other than Taty, all of my mom's siblings and family stayed, and died, in Cuba. Several of my cousins, sons and daughters of my mom's siblings, are still alive and living in Miami.

I also remember seeing my mom after she delivered my sister in Hawthorne. I was two years old at the time. Unky and Taty had brought my older sister and I to see my mom. We weren't allowed in the hospital room, so we stood outside and waved at my mom, who watched us from her hospital window. I remember crying because I missed my mom and wanted to be with her. I didn't like being without her, even at that young age, she was my comfort.

My mom's nephew (my cousin), Angel Hernandez, and his family witnessed some of my mom's abuse and isolation under guardianship. They were also isolated and restricted from seeing my mom by the guardians. My mom and her nephew were more like brother and sister because they grew up in the same blended household. He and his wife (Rosie) were both near 80 years old when my mom's guardianship began in 2011. My cousin, his wife, and their two children, and grandchildren were not allowed to visit or

speak to my mom unless the guardian had advance notice of their visit. The visit had to be approved in advance, and as with any scheduled visits, the guardian could refuse to allow them (anyone) in the facility when they arrived. Due to some of their medical issues, they could not give advanced notice. They needed their doctor's approval to travel. Another one of My mom's cousins who lived in New Jersey, talked to my mom every day when she was still in her home. She was also not allowed to speak to my mom. My mom's niece, could not visit or speak to my mom unless closely monitored. The only way my mom's family and close friends spoke to my mom, was when I called them on <u>my</u> cell phone at the lock down facilities. Everyone visiting my mom had to sign in/out. When my mom's phone was disconnected and a private line put in its place, while she still lived at home, she was cut off from dozens of people including those in her prayer groups, friends and family in Miami, as well as her church family and friends here in Gainesville, and New Jersey. No court orders were ever issued for these restrictions, other than setting visitation times for me and my sisters. However, my sisters would always come and go as they pleased.

The Cuban and The Italian Meet

In the beginning there was my mom and dad. It was a love story more wonderful than anything I had ever seen in a movie.

This was real life.

They were my parents.

They met in July 1956 on Miami Beach, Florida, outside the Bancroft Hotel beach side. My mom was literally swimming in the water. When she came out of the water, she saw some friends standing on the shore. And there was my dad. My mom always told me that all she saw was his piercing, beautiful blue eyes. She got lost in them. My dad was an amazing man, a WWII Navy Veteran. He was Sicilian Italian, and one VERY good looking man. He was raised Catholic, of course. No respectable Italian would be anything other than Catholic.

It was love at first sight.

My mother would always tell me, "he asked me if I was Latin, and I said, 'Latin, no, I'm CUBAN." My mother was an incredibly

devout Catholic. She was
drop dead gorgeous, but
her heart and soul were just
as beautiful. I remember my
Taty telling me more than
once that my mom had
"above and beyond" the
spirituality and devotion to
God than anyone else in

their family. My mom would teach catechism in Cuba and visited sick children in the hospital. She really did 'walk the walk, and talk the talk'. This never changed until the day she died. My mom often told me that she wanted to be a nun, but wasn't blessed enough to have the calling. We had this trait of spirituality in common as well, but I could never hold a candle to my mom. Ever.

My dad asked her out on a date immediately, but my mom told him the only place she would go out alone with him was to church. I have a picture of their first date, outside St. Patrick's Church on Miami Beach. She loved to tell this story, and I never got tired of hearing it. My dad proposed about two weeks later at the end of their vacations. He told my mom that he had been looking his entire life for her. My mom told him that he would have to marry her in Cuba, and in turn, she would have to live in New Jersey. I never remember my dad showing any disrespect toward my mom, and I always remember them hugging, kissing and loving each other.

He was all about her, and to love her was to love him.

They had their discussions, and sometimes they raised their voices, but they always ended up laughing and hugging. He did tease her, but my mom never took it seriously. My mom had this infectious laugh. When she got started, she couldn't stop. It was her way of always dealing with my dad when he got "grouchy" (as she would say). She passed that ability to laugh onto me, and in turn, I passed that onto my three girls. It was the kind of laugh where you can't breathe, and everyone else around you laughs along with you.

Many years later, and before my mother was placed into guardianship, I asked her about those last few trips to Cuba with my dad, my older sister and I before the Revolution. There is a 21-month difference between me and my older sister. I remember asking my mom that since they had been in Cuba when my sister was about 1 year old, could it be possible that I was conceived in Cuba on this trip? I remember my mom's face light up when I asked her this question. She looked at me with a gleam in her eye. I'll never forget that look. She smiled and said, "I think you're right!" Then she laughed. We both laughed. I guess that's probably why I always felt different, and why my mom and I were always so close – emotionally, spiritually, and physically. Our energy transcended time and place.

One of the reasons that I knew, and suspected, what was going on with her under guardianship was because I felt it in my heart and gut. Numerous times, I felt physical pain, and I know that many of these times coincided with the times she had fallen and was injured. I would also wake up from a deep sleep and call out for my mom. Many times, I had this sense of dread that something was happening to her.

I was always right.

My parents were so much in love. They oozed it. She was his everything, and he completed her. To know him, was to know her, and vice versa. You could not love one and not the other. Growing up, my dad demanded the utmost respect from his children toward their mother. This was how it was supposed to be. He was the most rugged, active, and outdoorsy man I ever knew. He loved being out in the country. He loved his family, especially his grandchildren.

My Dad Was My Hero

I'm not just saying "my dad was my hero" just like many sons and daughters say about their dad. My dad was a special kind of hero.

My dad served in the Navy during WWII. He was a Seaman First Class. He was not drafted, but in fact volunteered to fight for our country because it meant that much to him. His brother, my uncle Frank, was drafted and served in Guam. My dad left New Jersey and flew to California to await his orders.

The first time my dad spoke about his time in the Navy was after I had my second daughter. He told me that he was supposed to be sent to Pearl Harbor, but they delayed his orders. I tried to verify this information after he passed, but could never find anything that supported this statement. However, instead of Pearl Harbor, my dad was sent to the Solomon Islands on the *U.S.S. Quincy*. The Battle of Guadalcanal, code-named Operation Watchtower, was one of the first victories in the Pacific for the U.S. forces. It wasn't until I saw a documentary on the History Channel that I learned about the casualties suffered by the U.S. Navy and Marines in this battle at sea.

In the early morning of August 7, 1942, the attack on the Island of Guadalcanal and other surrounding islands began. The *U.S.S. Quincy* was hit by the Japanese, and sunk to the bottom of the ocean. About two-thirds of my dad's ship mates died. When my dad spoke about his horrific experience, his voice was sad and strained. I don't really think that he had spoken to too many people about it. I know he never really spoke much to my mom about it. I felt lucky to hear some of his story.

I asked him about that day, and this was almost exactly what he said, "I was handing the shells to the gunner, as they were bombing us. I turned around, just looked over my shoulder, and saw my captain being blown up to pieces. I didn't stop. I couldn't stop. I kept handing over the shells. When the ship sunk, we all swam. We all tried to grab life vests if we could. There was this one kid, he couldn't swim, so I gave him my vest. I knew how to swim." I listened intently to my dad's story. In my naïveté, I asked him what I thought was a poignant question, "but daddy, weren't you worried about the sharks when you were swimming." He responded, "sweetie, the sharks were the least of our worries." Obviously, with Japanese planes attacking the U.S. ships by air, dead bodies all around him, a battle raging on the island close by, and in the sea around them, I guess he was right. The sharks were the least of his worries. It was many hours before my dad was plucked from the waters and taken on another ship to safety. He was taken back to recuperate on a base off the coast of California. He never went out and saw combat again, but he served his five years in the Navy. My dad never got a medal for his heroism, for saving another man's life. But he was and will always be my hero.

The sad part about my dad's story, who was only 20 years old when he enlisted and traveled thousands of miles from his home to defend our country and our freedom, was that my mom lost all her freedom and rights under guardianship here in the U.S. I find that extremely ironic.

My dad spent about three months or so at sea, in the hull of the *U.S.S. Quincy*, he slept mostly in a hammock, in an enclosed room, with exposed pipes that were insulated with asbestos. My dad died from lung cancer due to asbestos exposure at the age of 78 – pleural mesothelioma. No one in our family ever died that young. I know things would have been different had my dad been alive.

But more about that later.

His untimely death played a large role in the family dynamics.

When my dad passed in 1999, I thought my mom would die after him. She got pneumonia the week after he died, and I almost lost her too. He was always on her mind. When we found out that my dad was sick and had terminal lung cancer, we decided as a family that they would all move up to Gainesville – my mom, dad, aunt and uncle. He died the week that the foundation on the house was being poured. He never made it up to Gainesville. My mom brought his ashes with her.

Two days before my mom died, I dreamt that my dad was lying next to her in the nursing home bed, and he was kissing her forehead. He had waited so long to be with her again, and I was grateful he had come to take her away from the suffering and abuse.

We Moved South

There were no changes of seasons in Miami, Florida. The seasons include hot, sweaty, sticky, and buggy. I saw roaches and Palmetto bugs the size of bats.

Moving from my small town in Paterson to a large city like Miami was scary for a fat little kid. The food was different, the city went at a faster pace, and there were so many more people and cars. However, there was the beach. I know that my parents struggled financially for a while in Miami, but they made things work.

We always had love, food on the table, and a roof over our heads. I know that my Taty and Unky helped them financially when they could. That was what family did – they helped each other.

I always went to Catholic schools, and while I missed my friends in Jersey, I knew that my parents were making HUGE sacrifices. My mom pushed me to excel academically, but my heart was into sports. I was a daydreamer. I always drew horses, and made my parents take us on trail rides before all the trees were cut down in Miami. I also learned how to play violin. My uncle taught me how to play classical violin, and he also taught me how to play tennis. He was a task master. I regret not keeping up with the violin. I stopped at about age 11, when I started playing sports. However, both my dad and uncle were both very much into sports, and I was really good at any sport.

During my formative years, they called it being "picked on" but today they call it bullying. Whatever it was called, it happened to me. I hate to admit it, but I did a little bit of bullying myself, which didn't feel right, so I stopped immediately, even if the person I was picking on had already been mean to me. As kids, we played, and we didn't complain or whine. It was handled amongst ourselves.

My childhood in Miami was pretty uneventful, well except for the fractured ankle and the tumor. At 13, I was playing in a softball tournament, and slid into home plate. And yes, I was safe. I twisted and fractured my left ankle. When the doctors looked at the X-ray, they saw that I had a tumor between my calf and ankle. It was a calcification, and I still have it to this day.

I did the usual preadolescent and teenage things. When I was about 14, we moved to a bigger house in the subdivision of Westchester (Miami). I went to an all-girl Catholic high school. My parents had scrimped and saved for years to get to a better place. My Taty and Unky moved in the house right next to us, and we had a very large yard. My mom started working as a substitute teacher when I was almost finished with high school and I had already bought my first car. I started working at 14. I had my first boy crush, puppy love, at 14.

I made friends pretty quickly and easily as a child. My mom always told me that I was a social butterfly like her. I still have some of those friends from elementary and high school today. My mom was happy being back with her family, friends and around her culture. My mom and I truly bonded over our love of Cuban music, the food, the coffee, the language, the weekly high school dances, and "los quinces." Quinces are like a "Sweet 16," but Hispanic teenagers celebrate at age 15 instead of 16.

Quince means 15 in Spanish. Quinces are elaborate parties. The birthday girl is treated like a debutante and there is dancing, sit down dinners, and a lot of presents. It was during these years in Miami that I would hear how similar in looks and personality my mom and I were. There was always this connection and understanding between us. I never felt the need to lie or deceive my mom or dad, as many teenagers do. She somehow knew what I was doing before I did it. She always told me that I was the easiest child. I never wanted to hurt her or my dad. I only wanted their love and approval.

Having three daughters of my own now, I somewhat understand that inner voice in a mother-daughter relationship. I could never be the mother that my mom was. To me, she was perfect, even though she had imperfections. I also gained a sense about my dad's upbringing during my teenage years, his history in the Navy and how he grew up as a child. I knew that the divorce of his parents weighed heavily on him. He never spoke much about his dad, who never stayed in touch with his children, after his parents divorced. My dad was a very "hands on" father. Even though he always worked hard, he had time for his children – he bathed us, played with us, cooked for us, and disciplined us.

But no one told me about "chaperoning." In the Cuban culture, as well as many other cultures, it is important for the young lady to attend social events, but they always had to be accompanied by a chaperone. The chaperone was usually female, a family member or close friend, and they watched that young lady like a hawk. I honestly think that the concept of a chaperone was more for the benefit and socialization of the actual person chaperoning than it was for watching the young ladies, and keeping their innocence intact.

After I bought my first car at age 16, I drove my mom everywhere. It really took a huge burden off my dad's shoulders because he was still working full time. My older sister moved to Iowa a month before her 18th birthday. It broke my mother's heart. She was devastated that my sister moved so far away. My mom and dad, and aunt and uncle helped my sisters in many ways during their college years and beyond – with school, tuition, books, food, and rent. Since I put myself through school and married young, I never asked my parents or godparents (aunt and uncle) for anything until much later in my life. Until after I got my divorce, I was always helping them.

My younger sister and her husband had a huge wedding in Miami. My dad took out a large loan to pay for this wedding. My older sister had a smaller wedding, but again, my dad paid for the wedding. I paid for both my weddings – by the justice of the peace and my church wedding. My parents also gave them personal loans, including a large home loan. I never got involved with what happened between my parents and my siblings, even though my mom always told me what was going on. It was none of my business and it was disrespectful to discuss it. I never asked "where is my share" or "how do we make it even." I wasn't raised that way by my parents.

At 18, I registered at a local community college and graduated with an AA less than two years later. I decided to apply to the University of Florida journalism department. Three months before I left Miami for Gainesville, and less than a week after her high school graduation, my younger sister headed for Gainesville herself. She had no plan, but to come and have a good time. She fell asleep at the wheel as she arrived in Gainesville, and totaled her car. She eventually got her RN from a local college, which was also paid for by my aunt and uncle.

During the time I was in community college, my mom and I went to a lot of social events, mostly involving her friends. But, if I would go out with my friends, I would let her know where I was and oftentimes called her from the party. I knew she would worry, and she always stayed up waiting for me. Years later, and even after I was married and had children, my mom would still wait up for me. She never stopped being a mom.

I left Miami for school in Gainesville, where several part time jobs awaited me. I graduated in 1981 with my bachelor's degree in Journalism. The year before I left Miami, I met the man who would eventually be my husband and father to my three children – William Lyles. Within a few months after leaving Miami, he followed me and came to live with me in Gainesville. We got married the following year, and divorced in 2004. We had three beautiful daughters.

My mom and dad were against the "living together" part. I think it broke both their hearts because they expected more of me, they had different expectations of what my love life and marriage would be like. It hurt not speaking to my parents for many months after they found out. I had never lied or deceived them. However, my parents learned to accept Bill, and three years later we had our first child. They became grandparents, a joy that changed all our lives. I had the first two grandchildren, two girls.

I remember when I first found out I was pregnant with my oldest daughter. The first person I called was my mom. I cried, and she cried with me. I would call her almost every day and tell her that I loved her and that I was sorry for anything I had done to hurt her. She would laugh and tell me I was the good child. I always felt like I was her favorite.

No one warned me what labor was really like. And yet, I did it two more times. I always wanted six children, but due to financial and other marital issues, three was my perfect number. I had three girls, just like my mom and dad.

We all began to prepare for her birth. I had chosen to have my first child at a local birthing center, which ended up being a big mistake. After 30+ hours of labor, my oldest daughter came into this world screaming. After several hours of being in the hospital and separated from her due to some complications from the birth, I was back home with my newborn baby girl and husband. My daughter was born with a full head of thick black hair. She was gorgeous, and she was perfect. I, on the other hand, was a hot mess. I could barely walk.

My parents left Miami the following day at 6 a.m. for the journey to see their first grandchild. While I was still in labor, my sisters had called my parents, and then again the minute after my daughter was born. My mom told me that when my dad heard that she was a beautiful, perfectly healthy baby girl, he broke down and cried like a baby himself. I knew my mom had been praying the entire time. My mother also had a very difficult first labor. My middle child was the easiest labor, as was I.

I will never forget the look on my parents face when they saw their first grandchild for the first time. My dad immediately scooped her up from the basinet and took her in his arms. He kissed her little hands and feet, and then handed her to my mom, who was already sitting in the rocking chair waiting. I laid in bed, barely able to move, wondering when they would eventually get around to noticing me!!!

The first five months or so after my daughter was born, my Taty and mom stayed with me, alternating their visits. They helped to cook, clean and take care of my daughter. When I went back to work, they stayed with my daughter for another month before she went into daycare. This was repeated with each of my children, as well as each of their other grandchildren. My parents, and aunt and uncle, were pivotal in raising and forming the personalities of my three children. In their later years, my daughters were always there to assist and help them, especially my mom whom they adored. Nine grandchildren were born, with the youngest born about three weeks after my dad passed in 1999. My oldest daughter could not say "abuelita," which means grandmother in Spanish, so everyone called her "Lita," and my dad was "Pappa."

CHAPTER 3

The Road to Guardianship – How Did We Get Here?

When I began to think back about the "warning signs" of discord in my family, I could probably go into early childhood. I remember the typical parent-daughter disagreements between my parents and my siblings, mostly my oldest sister. There were occasions both siblings were disrespectful to my parents, and as I said, I never felt the need to lie or deceive them, regardless if they disagreed with my choices. I always listened and respected them.

My older sister would often bring my mom to tears with her unkind words and biting remarks, and my dad did not take kindly to the disrespect. I believe this was the source of discord between them, but whenever my sister needed my parents, they were always there for her.

For many years, I knew that I would probably be the one who took care of my mom and dad, and aunt and uncle, as they got older. I remember always telling my mom, "don't worry, you'll be with me. I'll never put you in a home." We use to joke that we would buy a big house and live there with my kids, husband, animals, and mom and dad. I always honored my parents in every way I could. At age 16, after my first "big" paycheck, I bought my parents a new family room set, which included a couch, a loveseat and a single chair. My parents cried tears of joy. It was the first of many presents that I gave my parents over the years.

My dad passed away on September 5, 1999. He died of respiratory arrest from lung cancer due to pleural mesothelioma. Evidently, he had been living with severe chest pain for years. He had complained of arthritis, but no one realized how serious it was until early 1999.

In February 1999, shortly before his 78th birthday, my dad doubled over in pain, he was holding his chest. My mom thought he was having a heart attack. She called us immediately. X-rays showed a mass in his lungs, and they diagnosed him with lung cancer. His biopsy in May confirmed his diagnosis. It was Stage IV lung cancer. I drove to Miami for his biopsy with my oldest daughter, then 15. When I spoke to the oncologist, he said that his cancer was so severe that it had eaten away at several ribs. The doctor told me that he did not understand how my dad had endured the pain for so long. Over the next few months, my dad received massive doses of radiation. My uncle drove him to all his appointments. My mom was always by his side. My dad tried to stay positive. My mom did not believe he would die. This was her best friend and her soul mate. But I think she knew it was inevitable.

During my dad's illness, I spoke to my parents every day. I had heart to heart talks with my mom, and I knew that it was extremely difficult for her to deal with so much. She would cry sometimes, but mostly she prayed for a miracle.

As a family, we made the decision that my parents, and aunt and uncle should move to Gainesville for my dad's treatment, and be surrounded by his children and grandchildren during his last months. I was given the task of being the liaison between my uncle and the real estate company who was building the homes.

My dad was getting weaker.

He was giving up.

In July, we decided that all three children should start helping my parents pack for the move. One sister had already been to Miami the week prior to my arrival. The first thing I noticed was how skinny and worn my dad looked. He had a lot of trouble breathing. He was angry at his disability. My youngest daughter was almost 4 then, but he could not pick her up or play outside with her. I knew they were both disappointed. Even though she was so young, to this day, my youngest daughter remembers so much about her papa – the way he felt, the way he laughed, and the way he held her hand so tightly.

No one had talked to my dad about death and dying until I got there that July weekend. No one had talked to him about his fears and anxieties surrounding death. No one had told him that he was terminal and dying. But he knew. He wasn't ready to accept it yet. He was angry, mostly because he couldn't play with his grandchildren. He ranted about feeling out of breathe walking from the bedroom to the kitchen, and not being able to make my mom her morning coffee. He was mad about losing his independence. I listened to him and tried not to cry. All I could say was that I loved him. I remember telling him, "if you don't feel like fighting anymore, that's ok, you don't have to. If you don't feel like doing the radiation anymore, that's ok, you don't have to." No one had told him he had choices. I know my mom kept pushing for treatment because she didn't want to lose him.

My task was to clean out the garage. This was no small task. I asked my dad to move his car into the driveway and out of the garage and he asked me why. I told him that I wanted to pack up some boxes and clean out the garage for the move. He told me there was nothing to clean. I did not disrespect him, but simply told him that I would work around his car, even though it would take longer for me to pack boxes. Less than two minutes later, while I was putting on my work clothes, I heard him move the car from the garage into the driveway. Three hours later, the garage was done. He beamed with pride and thanked me profusely. He loved it. My mom told me how happy I had made him. I knew I was going to lose my dad, but like my mom, I kept praying and never gave up hope. He is the reason that I decided to study health education and get my Ph.D. I'll never forget what my dad told me years earlier, when I made the decision to get my master's degree, "do what makes you happy, Tess."

Only my dad and my uncle were allowed to call me Tess.

Before my July visit, I tried to gain as much knowledge as I could about mesothelioma. I saw some law offices listed on the internet in Miami, and I contacted one of them about my father's condition. They were eager to take my dad's case, and asked if I would videotape my father during my July visit for testimony. I explained to my father about the disease and the lawsuit. He did not want to be video recorded, and I had to abide by his wishes.

My dad collapsed for the first time in mid-August. The hospital wanted him to drink that horrible liquid so that they could place a scope up his anus. He kept refusing. This was the first time that I remember my mom sounding desperate and angry at him during the entire illness. I told my dad that he didn't have to drink the liquid or agree to the procedure. He came home and was there for about a week, then he collapsed again for the last time. My mom called me at home. It was my oldest daughter's 16th birthday. I had about 30 people in my house for her party. But my mom was crying and telling me that they had put tubes in my dad and she couldn't handle this alone. He was in the Intensive Care Unit. She said to me, "I'm going to lose him. I'm going to lose my life." My sisters and I drove down early the next day.

I wasn't prepared to see my dad dying.

When I saw my mom, she looked tired, sick, sad, and depressed. She told me after my dad died that she had begun to bleed vaginally during those last weeks of his life. She was 80.

When I walked into the room, I didn't recognize my dad. He was lying in the bed, his skin looked gray and he was very thin. He opened his eyes, and I saw that he was intubated. With his hands he signaled a cutting motion toward the tubes in his mouth. I shook my head and let him know that I understood. I fought back tears, but I took his hand and began to do the only thing that came naturally to me. I began to pray with him. They had put restraints on his wrists and ankles because he had tried to pull out the tubes. His wrists and ankles were bruised. My mom did not want to sign the Do Not Resuscitate (DNR) order. I was left with the task of convincing my mom that this was the right thing to do for my dad.

How do you convinced a woman to let go of a man that had protected, loved, supported, and denied her nothing for 43 years? How do you explain to your own mom that her husband does not want to live the remaining weeks of his life intubated? How do you ask your mom to let go of the only man she has ever loved? How do I find the strength to ask her to let my dad go to God?

I spent that night in the hospital, sleeping in the waiting room so that my mom could have some rest. She was emotionally and physically exhausted. The next day, my mom signed the DNR orders. We were able to make my dad smile and laugh, and I promised him that he wouldn't have to suffer much longer. He knew.

We left that afternoon and drove back to Gainesville. Two days later, my mom called again. They were going to take his tubes out, and she needed us to be there. They had tried to wean him off the respirator, but it had not gone well. I drove down to Miami again, this time with only my older sister. Labor Day weekend was a few days away.

I was in the room when they removed my dad's tubes, along with my sister and a priest. My mom told me that she couldn't watch him die, and I understood. I was prepared for him to go quickly, but instead, his gray and ashen face immediately regained its color. I could hear him take one deep breath and sigh. He was transformed. A sense of peace came over him, his cheeks were pink. The priest called my mother into the room and told her, "look at what just happened!" We waited, 30 minutes, then an hour, then two hours. I asked the ICU nurse if we could get a private room. She told me that they were all booked, but within 15 minutes, she received a call that a room had just become available. He was up in the private room within minutes. We continued to wait. I spent that night with my dad in that private room. My mom went home to sleep. She looked defeated.

I had the strangest dreams that night. It didn't even feel like I was dreaming. I felt like I was conscious, but transported to the ceiling of the room, hovering across to where my dad was sleeping and into his chest. The cancer was black and it had consumed his body. It scared me.

My dad was still alive 24 hours after they extubated him, and I now faced a dilemma. Should I stay with my mom, which I really wanted to do, or return home with my sister? My mom and I found ourselves alone in the private room – just me, her and my dad.

I remember kneeling with my head on her lap, crying and telling her that I wanted to stay and be with her and my dad. I will never forget what she said to me that morning, "my daughter, you should go back with your sister, because if anything would happen to her on the drive back, I could never forgive myself for asking you to stay." I did what my mom asked, but I had this sick feeling in my stomach. Before I left, I whispered something in my dad's ear, "Daddy, I promise I'll take care of mommy." I kept this promise until June 2011, when my mom was taken into guardianship.

My dad died at about 3 am on the following day. My mom was lying in the bed next to him when he passed. My aunt called me at about 5 am to give me the news. I drove down later that morning with my husband and three children. I was the only one who went to his funeral.

The funeral was exhausting, because I was trying to focus on my mom. The night that I arrived, I slept with my mom in the spot that use to be my dad's. She was burning up with fever. I was scared. A few days after I left, and after I made my uncle take my mom to the doctor, I found out that she had double pneumonia. I couldn't lose them both, not in such a short period of time. I prayed harder for her recovery.

My mom recovered slowly and in December 1999, we moved my aunt, uncle, and mom to their new homes in Gainesville. Our families were all centrally located near Gainesville, or we worked and went to school in Gainesville. We all had easy access to my mom, aunt and uncle. I took my mom and aunt numerous times back to Miami for vacation and visits with their friends and family. The last time I drove my mom and aunt back there was in 2009.

Within a month after my father's death, I began to work with the Miami law firm on filing multiple law suits for my dad's wrongful death. My mom was reluctant to proceed because she was still grieving, and my siblings did not want to participate at all in the process. It took many months to get all the paperwork to the law firm. Within a year, they had filed 27 separate law suits on my dad's behalf for asbestos exposure, starting with his time in the Navy on the *U.S.S. Quincy*. By late 2000, my mom had started to receive checks from the law suit. She was shocked and surprised. She told me that she wanted to give me half of all the money she received because I had done all the work and spent so much of my time on this endeavor. I told her that she needed to put most of it away for a nest egg, because more was coming, and that this was my dad's way of taking care of her. My mom decided to periodically give her three children and grandchild monetary gifts. She always wanted to give me more, but I told her that we should all get the same amount. She would always ask me, "what should I give your sisters," and my answer would be the same, "it has to be equal."

My mom never got a chance to live the last four years of her life comfortably. When she was forced into guardianship, she had more than enough money to live the rest of her life in her home.

The last four years of her life, she never saw one cent of her own money.

The last four years of her life, she lived with constant drugging.

The last four years of her life, she lived in poverty, in pain, with strangers, and isolated from her family, her church and her friends.

Making My Way

My family was broken by guardianship.

The effect of my mom's imprisonment into guardianship did not just affect my family, our children, my cousins, and their children, but it also affected a community of friends, colleagues, my mom's friends and their family in Miami, New Jersey, Gainesville, and other communities. My mom had so many friends who loved her. She touched the lives of so many people. Everyone was affected by her isolation and restrictions. In total, I would estimate that at least three dozen friends, family, and church (spiritual) friends were affected by her imprisonment and isolation under guardianship, but it is hard to estimate the total.

My sisters could have stopped this at any time, but they did not.

I started my master's degree in 1989, and finished in 1994. I went back for my doctorate in 2001. I got divorced in 2004, while more than half-way through my doctoral program. I was also starting menopause with a vengeance, and making about $12,000 a year teaching. The divorce had been a long time coming.

The divorce left me in emotional, spiritual, and financial ruin. I received little to no child support for almost six years. When he died in 2012, the father of my children owed me almost $60,000 "on the books" – what the court recorded as being owed. However, from 2004 to 2012, he rarely, if ever, had visitations with my underage daughter(s), which meant no weekends, and no monetary support during that time. I was a 100% full-time parent. I estimated that he owed me close to $100,000 of which I could never recover. I went to court more than two dozen times to request child support. It was pointless.

The divorce took its toll on me and my children.

My mom, aunt, and uncle stepped up and helped me financially during the next few years, mostly to pay my electric and food bills, and help with any school supplies and expenses for my youngest daughter. They also helped take care of my youngest daughter while I was in class and during my data collection and dissertation writing. However, they also helped all the other grandchildren as well.

I had never asked my parents for any substantial amount of money until now. I had supported myself since even before I left Miami for the University of Florida in Gainesville, and even after I got married.

I struggled with depression before, during and after the divorce, but I never stopped working multiple jobs. I took a low paying job with insurance immediately after I graduated with my doctorate, then transitioned to a higher paying job within a few months. My income did not meet my expenses. My mom, aunt and uncle continued to me help financially. But I also continued to help them.

I was at my mom's house a lot because I needed to be around her. I needed her hugs, her kisses and her prayers. I would often fall asleep with her in the same bed because I was always so physically exhausted. Because I had never depended on her, nor asked, for financial help, this bothered me more than the emotional and financial roller coaster I was experiencing. Some weeks I felt that I could not focus or concentrate on even the simplest tasks. I had too much going on and was pulled in 1,000 different directions.

However, from 1999 to 2010, I found the time to take my mom and aunt to Miami many times over. They visited their friends, and I drove them wherever they wanted to go. Most of the time, I also had my children with me. The trips back to Miami were a joy for them, and it allowed me to see a side of these sisters that I hadn't seen before. These trips were so much fun and interesting, and they had so much love for each other. I felt honored to share these times with them.

During this time, my uncle's vision problems progressed and he stopped driving. They took cabs on occasion, but mostly I drove them to church, grocery shopping and out to eat. Even though I was struggling to stay afloat, and was emotionally burdened, I felt that they had done so much for me for so long, and I was happy to oblige them.

In June 2007, my uncle had a massive stroke and died within a week. My aunt became a shell of her former self. In October 2007, at their request, I took my mom and aunt to make their wills. I tried to take care of both women as best I could, but given my financial circumstances, it was difficult to support my family and care for them as well.

Within a year after my uncle's death, my sisters began talking about placing both of them in nursing home facilities. I vehemently opposed. They called "family meetings" and they began their pressure tactics.

The Root of All Evil – Pre-Guardianship-The Pressure Begins

"The seven deadly sins are pride, greed, lust, envy, gluttony, wrath and sloth."

Greed, envy, pride, and wrath play the most important roles in guardianship of an elder. The seeds had been planted for many years.

In 2009, my old car gave out. I was left without a vehicle for work and taking my daughter to school. I felt overwhelmed and frustrated. I felt like no matter how hard I worked, I could not get ahead. I decided to move in with my mom, with her permission, and try to save some money. I was not sure what I would do with my house. I couldn't think that far ahead. I couldn't think.

I began looking for a new vehicle. My mom offered to give me a loan to buy a truck. We agreed on a payment plan that included some bartering and biweekly monetary payments. Several years later (August 1, 2012), the first plenary guardian, filed a "Subpoena Duces Tecum Without Deposition to Susan Johnson of Park Motor Group" to acquire a copy of the title for my vehicle. I guess she felt that if my mom was listed on the title of my truck, she could legally take and sell it, and keep the funds. One of dozens of frivolous motions that had nothing to do with my mom's best interest.

During the six months or so that my youngest daughter and I lived with my mom, I paid for most of the groceries, the cable bill, and some of the electric bill. I also took my aunt and mom to most, if not all, of their medical appointments. I started out with giving my mom bank checks for truck payments, but soon discovered that she would rip them up. Instead, I would hide money in her purse and dresser drawers so that she would not know where it came from. Unfortunately, this tactic to pay my mom came back to bite me in the butt because I had no formal record of how much money I actually gave back. In the end, after all the food, caregiving, medical trips, and vacations I spent out of pocket, with my mom and aunt, exceeded what the guardians and my siblings thought that I had borrowed or been given as "gifts" from my mom.

When I moved out from my mom's home, I rented a place in the country. But after about eight months there, I decided to move back to my own house. These moves were part of a very stressful and painful journey. I realized that I had a long way to financial recovery. I also realized how much uprooting I did with my youngest daughter, and how much I put my family through. I felt like I was in a row boat lost in a huge ocean. I wasn't myself and I wasn't thinking straight. I made some bad decisions. The emotional and physical pain continued.

Then my sisters found out about the truck loan.

The seeds of greed and envy had begun.

The spiral toward guardianship had started.

During the next few years, the strain in our family intensified, mostly due to the decisions made about where my aunt and mom should reside. I was accused of taking my mom's money numerous times. There were numerous angry emails, accusations, and finger pointing. However, the gifts (checks) that my mom gave them from the law suit funds, I had filed, were taken by my sisters with no qualms.

As early as May 26, 2010, my older sister began to plant the seeds of my mom needing medical attention by inventing illnesses:

"I just talked to mom. I'm pretty sure that she had a serious TIA yesterday. She described these symptoms: severe headache that was extremely painful, weakness and numbness on her left side. I offered to pay her taxi. I know if you encourage her, she'll do it."

A TIA or Trans Ischemic Attack is also called a "mini-stroke." TIAs are caused by temporary blockage of blood flow, usually through a clot. Symptoms of a TIA are similar as a stroke. They include numbness, tingling, weakness, and loss of movement in the face, arm or leg, suddenly having difficulty speaking, confusion, and balance issues (walking).[2] Obviously my mom was not having a TIA; however, TIA's were one of the supposed diagnoses my mom had during the time she was under guardianship.

In 2010 without consulting with me, my sisters convinced my mom's primary care physician that she needed home health, but they refused to be an active part of the process. They put me down as the primary contact without consulting me. I was constantly being called away from work to meet the physical therapist, occupational therapist and home health nurse at my mom's home.

After several weeks, and multiple conflicts with my mom's appointments, mostly due to numerous other appointments being made without telling me, I asked my sisters to take over as primary contact for the home health people. I felt I had done my part and now it was their turn. They refused, and accused me of "firing" the home health agency, which can only be done by the primary care physician. I suggested that we try this again, but as I stated above, I asked to be contacted only in case of emergency, for our adult

---

[2] http://www.webmd.com/stroke/tc/transient-ischemic-attack-tia-topic-overview

children to help, and for my two siblings to be the primary contacts since they were the ones pushing for this.

On June 24, 2010, after my younger sister kept insisting that we should "meet with a social worker b/c (sic) they would be able to help us with options," and "...I think with mom's confusion and agitation it would help us coordinate everything." I responded in an email to my two sisters stating:

> "My daughter is going to be living there in another month. Frankly, I think mom is pretty functional and it is the APPROACH to asking mom for medical attention. Dr. Velazquez wants her to reap the benefits of the home care agency, and agrees the social worker should WAIT until we actually follow through with the OT, PT, and home health nurse FIRST. You and Carmen were the ones pressing for this, so you have to follow through. I've already done my part, and so have my children. If you, Carmen, Paul, and your adult children are NOT willing to participate, then everything is pointless. This is about what we can do for mom, how we can help her, what is best for her, and how we can transition all these changes in HER life, not OUR life.
> Yes, it will be a bit disruptive to some of our lives, but you know what, big deal.....we have to be patient and understanding to mom's needs. If we aren't, she will refuse. We have to first and foremost be respectful of her space. Would you like someone to come barging in your home and say, 'OK, we're going to do this, this and this?' I think not. She is elderly, and we need to work with her as best as we can. Let me know when you plan on scheduling the meeting for our family."

The meeting with the social worker never happened. I refused to be used as a pawn and manipulated to be the "bad guy" in the scenario when they were not helping.

I felt I wasn't being a good parent, good daughter, niece, friend, or employee. I hated what was happening to me, inside and out during this time. I was always emotional, mostly due to the circumstances created that surrounded my mom, and also due to my unstable financial situation. I made bad decisions about my finances and people (men) in general. Even though I was a hard worker, I literally could not concentrate on even the simplest tasks at work. I would forget deadlines. I cried all the time, and lost my temper a lot at work, toward my children, and my friends.

My relationship with my children and close friends suffered. I began to isolate myself because I was afraid and distrustful. I fell in love with people who gave me nothing emotionally and spiritually, and who lied, cheated, abused, and disrespected me. I didn't care, because I was in so much emotional pain and felt so broken inside. The only thing that saved me from going completely mad was riding my horses, and staying in contact with the one or two friends that stood by me through the entire guardianship ordeal.

Regardless of my inner struggles and severe and debilitating bouts with depression, I still found the time to take my mom and aunt traveling to Miami and Orlando, and their medical appointments. They depended on me, and I had to do the best that I could for everyone. My daughters would jokingly tell me for years that I loved my mom more than I loved them.

My oldest daughter moved to North Carolina in 2010 with her fiancé, who was in the military. My middle daughter moved in with my mom in July 2010 to help care for her and my aunt, primarily to end the dispute about placing them in nursing homes. If my mom needed anything, my daughter would always call me.

During the time that my daughter lived with my mom, the four of us – my two youngest daughters, my mom and I – would always have Sunday dinner together. It was such a wonderful time. My aunt would often join us, but she was keeping more and more to herself. We always brought her food.

My aunt missed my uncle, and she started giving away her Christmas decorations and other belongings within a year after he died. I was worried about her. She got very sick with the stomach flu in December of 2010. I remember walking in her house and seeing that she had soiled her bed. I washed her bedding and clothes. She was very weak, but I nursed her back to health and checked on her several times a day. I asked my mom to do the say.

I spent the night at her house or my mom's house, so that I could keep an eye on her those first few days. I bought her Pedia-lite, and chicken broth. My sisters' response to her illness was that she needed "24 hour care." They never offered to help me or help her recuperate. They didn't want to be bothered with her either.

That Christmas, our last together as a family, I made the black beans and rice that had always been my aunt's task. It was the first time my aunt told me that they were "perfect. "

"Mommy I'm Scared"

During the late Summer and Fall of 2010, I noticed that my middle daughter kept getting ill with great frequency. In previous years, she had suffered a ruptured appendix, several bouts of pneumonia and a clot in her lungs at age 20. Now, at 24, she kept losing weight, was constantly lethargic, and kept getting sick. In January 2011, I took her to several specialists, including a hematologist, who diagnosed her with an immune disorder. About three weeks later, in the late evening hours of February 13th, while spending the night at my house, she asked me to take her to the Emergency Room at Shands in Gainesville. Within 30 minutes of arriving in the ER, I was asked to leave the room. The last thing I saw was the panic in my daughter's eyes – "mommy I'm scared."

Shortly after midnight on the 14th, the trauma doctors induced her into a coma and placed her on life support. I begged God to take me, but I got on my knees in that ICU room and prayed as hard as I could. I called my mom and my aunt, and they began a prayer chain for my daughter. My mother told me that God would save her. I tried with all my heart to believe her, and deep inside, I knew my mom was right.

My oldest daughter drove from North Carolina to Gainesville to be with us. On the third day my daughter was off life support. On the fourth day after her collapse, she asked for a cheeseburger. Her doctors were perplexed at her speedy recovery. They told me they could not understand why she was still alive. They told me it was a miracle.

My mom knew. She always knew.

During the next three weeks my daughter stayed in the hospital, first in ICU for a week, then in mid-level, and finally in regular care rooms. I had little to no time to spend attending to my mom and aunt's needs. I went from hospital, to my home, to my mom's home, and to work.

I didn't sleep.

My emotional and physical states were crashing.

The guardianship plan began to take shape.

The first few months after my daughter came home were critical. I drove her to all her doctor's appointments because she was unable to drive in her frail condition. She needed chemo infusions and constant blood tests. She went through dozens of medications. I could not think of anything else other than her survival and well-being. I stayed in touch with my mom every day, and would try to visit her at least every other day, if not every day. I also somehow found the energy and time to clean a little for her and make sure her and my aunt had groceries. My primary concern was my daughter, and my mom knew what I was going through. She understood.

During the last week of March 2011, my aunt suffered a stroke. She had not been feeling well for several months prior, and complained of having flu-like symptoms. I tried to make a doctor's appointment for her, but she refused to go, saying that she just needed to rest. I offered to take her multiple times.

The first night she was in the hospital, I stayed with her, and left my sick daughter at home. I was concerned and worried. Since I had worked with health care providers whose specialty were stroke survivors, I consulted with them on local rehabs. Less than a week after my aunt had her stroke, I visited her in the hospital, which I did almost every day. One of the nurses attending to her handed me an envelope with my older sister's name on it. She said, "this is the evaluation that you ordered." I wasn't sure what she meant, but she told me that my aunt had passed the competency exam with flying colors.

My mouth dropped.

My aunt had not even started rehab, speech therapy or even been discharged from the hospital.

Against my protests, my sisters placed my aunt in a local rehab facility. I was still dealing with my daughter's health and well-being. I thought they were acting in her best interest. This couldn't have been further from the truth.

Within the first week at the facility, my aunt developed bed sores on her butt, and fell several times. When I visited, I usually took my mom and daughters with me. When I noticed the bed sores, I told the nurses. They knew about them and the falls because they told me about some of her falls.

By April, I was at my wit's end. I was exhausted. I took a long weekend in mid-April and went camping with my youngest daughter. When I got back, I had a letter from the Department of Children and Families (DCF) waiting.

Department of Children and Families (DCF)

Five years after guardianship began, and reading about hundreds of cases and documents, I know that nothing is done by chance. Everything against the elder is planned and calculated.

I received the letter from DCF dated **April 16, 2011** stating that I "have been identified as a Possible Responsible Person for abuse, neglect or exploitation of a vulnerable adult."

The investigation for this first case was closed **June 10, 2011**, and my mom received a letter dated **June 9, 2011** stating that "no services recommended" for the accusations of abuse, neglect or exploitation.

Someone had called DCF claiming that I was stealing money, financially exploiting and abusing my mom, and that my mom was living in filth. In total, DCF was contacted three times by the same individual(s).

In this first DCF report, the accuser stated that my

mom,

> "has forgotten how to dial a phone and has put the phone in the refrigerator in the past," and continues, "Theresa Lyles is the daughter of Ms. Tozzo and her caregiver. Last summer the daughter fired social workers and other care providers that were coming into the home to provide care to Ms. Tozzo. At times Ms. Tozzo has been left alone. She is unable to walk and has fallen several times in the past. The caregiver has been leaving her daughter Barbara in the home on and off for a year to appear as if someone is in the home with Ms. Tozzo. Barbara has an illness and is bedridden; therefore she is unable to provide care for Ms. Tozzo.
>
> The condition of the home is a 'mess'. There are grease stains all over the carpet; there is no soap or toilet paper in the bathroom and there are plates of food in the bathroom.
>
> The caregiver has possession of Ms. Tozzo's credit card and is supposed to use the card to purchase groceries and other items for the home. The caregiver has used the credit card for personal use. 2 ½ years

ago, Ms. Tozzo allowed the caregiver to use 30,000 to buy a truck."

The DCF investigator report of the situation stated the following:

"The home is a house with vinyl siding, clean and without hazards on the outside. Inside was relatively clean; the carpet had spots on it and needed to be cleaned. All utilities were working, there was <u>food in the refrigerator</u> and cupboard, and no hazards or bad odors as noted. The VA stated that she does not have any disability and is able to perform all of her ADLs independently. She repeatedly asked 'Why are you here? Who sent you? Who called?' Her daughter, who is her primary CG and granddaughter see her almost every day.

Though V's home needed a more thorough cleaning, no evidence was found to support the allegation of environmental hazards. AP and her sisters were signatories on V's account until the date the guardian was appointed. It is not possible to determine exactly when V lost capacity. Therefore, API concluded that there are no indicators for the allegations of environmental hazards and inadequate supervision, **and the allegation of exploitation is not substantiated.**"

The first investigation took several months, but I was finally cleared of all charges. The other two did not even take a week. I was cleared on the other two charges as well. However, during those months during the first accusation and investigation, my life and my financial records were scrutinized. I could have lost my mom, my home, and my youngest daughter, who was then under age. I ended up losing my mom to guardianship anyway. These events also caused incredible stress on my family, especially my daughter who was still recovering from her near death encounter just a few months earlier. If things had not ended in a positive way, I could have lost custody of my youngest daughter, who was only 15 at the time. I could have lost my job, and my independence.

This is exactly what they wanted. They tried, but never did succeed.

I was interviewed for about two hours at the local DCF office after the first accusation. I was told by the agent that my mom could not be alone, and that my mom had to be kept clean and fed. I was told that if these demands did not happen, I would be in big trouble and legal action would be taken against me. I did not understand what this was all about. I pleaded my case. I cried. I was the one that had always taken care of my mom.

Why was this happening?

A multitude of my friends sent emails to the DCF investigator about my relationship with my mom and her treatment. Some of these friends knew my mom and I for more than 30 years. Some exerts of their statements include:

"I have known Teresa and her family since we met in 6th grade in school. Teresa has always put her family before anything in her life. Teresa is kind, patient and always loving and at the same time has taken her responsibility very serious. Teresa loves and respects her mother." (MG)

"To even imagine that Teresa is negligent or abusive to her mother is preposterous and evil. Teresa is definitely one of the most Loving people around. Teresa treats her mother with such sensitivity and sensibility that you have to constantly compliment her. Whoever filed this vile and vicious report about Teresa is a very twisted person and full of contempt, not only toward Teresa, but toward Mrs. Carmen Tozzo." (MSD)

"I have known Teresa since 1991, when we worked together at the University of Florida. The thing that has always stood out in my mind about Teresa has been her total commitment to her family – parents, siblings and children. I can think of no one who better exemplifies the concept of being a loving daughter than Teresa." (CHF).

"I have personally known Teresa for over 21 years and her mother, Carmen Tozzo, for over 12 years. Ms. Lyles is one of the most compassionate, empathetic, caring, and giving people I have ever known. She visits her mother at least once a day and is in contact with her almost every hour. She cleans her house and grocery shops for her, as well as sets her medications up for her on a regular basis. She is often shuttling her mother and her aunt to the doctor and dentist as well as the beauty shop and church. Please consider Carmen Tozzo in this case, as this is her home and her security you would be disrupting." (KSV)

"I have known her and her family for the past 20 years. I have never seen any abuse or neglect towards her by Teresa. Teresa is one of the most hardworking and honest people I know. I would trust her with anything." (KG)

DCF was contacted again on **May 13, 2011,** the day my aunt, Blanca Tozzo, came home from the assisted living facility. That investigation was closed on **May 19, 2011.**

The accusation included the following in this report: "On 5/13/2011, the niece removed Ms. Tozzo from her treatment facility. This is believed to have done for the niece to take advantage of her. Ms. Tozzo should have remained at the facility. There is also concern that the niece will try to take Ms. Tozzo's money. The niece is said to have taken over $40,000 from her mother."

I went from taking $30,000 to $40,000 in less than one month. This was just another attempt to keep me away from my mom and aunt.

The DCF investigator's final report for this accusation stated: "There is no credible evidence to support neglect. The AV (alleged victim) denied the allegation and said that she wanted to leave the NH (nursing home), recover at her home. The AP (alleged perpetrator) named in the report denies the allegation and said that she was just trying to do what her aunt wanted. She believes she is being harassed by another family member who wants control over the situation. ADON at Palm Gardens NH where AV was residing said that the AV wished to go home. Said AV felt out of place there with so many people who did not share her culture and language. AV was released with Dr. order for 24/7 home care. API observed the medical chart and found documentation that AV has capacity according to psychological report."

DCF should have prosecuted the person(s) who called for the second and third reports. DCF False Reporting Guidelines state that "any person who knowingly and willfully makes a false report or counsels another to make a false report is guilty of a felony of the third degree punishable by up to five years in prison. In addition, the department may impose a fine not to exceed $10,000 for each violation."

The third, and final DCF investigation was **August 15, 2011** and closed on **September 6, 2011.** The accusations for this last report was that I was "rough and aggressive" to my mom and caused her bruising.

For this report, I was accused of the following, "Theresa was rough with Mrs. Tozzo and left bruises on her. Theresa has also taken a large sum of money from Mrs. Tozzo."

My mom was already under the care of the first emergency guardian, who also controlled all of her money. The DCF investigator interviewed my mom in her home. When she saw him, my mom asked, "Why are you here." The report summary states:

"There is no credible evidence to support the allegations of Physical Injury and Exploitation. Collateral with paramour (lover) of APs sister revealed that he stated AP grabbed V's arm during an argument, causing a bruise. Stated he did not think this was intentional. He also stated that money AP allegedly took from V was before V had a plenary guardian appointed. (This allegation was investigated in a previous case.) This case is complete and closed, no indicator of Physical Injury and no indicator for exploitation."

Right after the first DCF report, I had to take my mom to her primary care physician for a check-up. My oldest daughter, my mom's designated health care surrogate went, as well as my oldest sister, who admitted inside the examining room that she was the one that had contacted DCF. I contacted DCF and reported her for filing a false report, which was done two more times. DCF did not take action.

During the entire guardianship, the threat of non-visitation was used as a form of emotional blackmail against me. They used the one thing that they knew would emotionally, physically and spiritually affect me – the health and well-being of my mom, and being able to see her.

Prior to the courts designating a temporary guardian, Monica Brasington, who was hired as an attorney by my siblings, filed the following :

On **April 28, 2011:**   "Petition to Determine Incapacity"
On **April 29, 2011:**

·   "Petition for Appointment of Limited and Standby Guardian."

·   "Oath of Guardian, Designation of Resident Agent and Acceptance"

·   "Application for Appointment as Guardian – Elena Clark"

The "Petition to Determine Incapacity" states that my sister Elena Clark, the petitioner, was a "son." It also further states that my sister:

"believes that Carmen Tozzo to be incapacitated…is physically and mentally unable to care for herself. She has been diagnosed with dementia and is unable to understand or manage her finances…the petitioner believes that the alleged incapacitated person is incapable of exercising the following rights: to have a driver's license, to seek/retain employment, to sue and defend lawsuits, to contract, to manage property or to make any gift of disposition of property, to determine her residency, to consent to medical/dental/surgical treatment, including psychiatric treatment."

Coincidentally, these were the SAME rights that the Examining Committee took away from my mom….about ONE MONTH later. They did not state "alleged incapacitated" person in this document. Obviously, my sister is not "a son." My mom had not been diagnosed with dementia at the time of this petition.

The "Petition for Appointment of Limited and Standby Guardian" names my sisters as proposed Guardian and Standby Guardian. In this document, it was stated that my mom, "alleged incapacitated person's alleged incapacity is suspected to be: dementia/Alzheimer's type." The petition also stated that: "it is necessary that a guardian be appointed to exercise the following delegable rights of the Ward as follows: to have a driver's license, to seek/retain employment, to sue and defend lawsuits, to contract, to manage property or to make any gift of disposition of property, to determine her residency, to consent to medical/dental/surgical treatment, including psychiatric treatment."

However, in this petition, it does state that my sister is "a daughter." They also stated the "nature and value of the property," which included $126,500 (property/home), $80,470.71 (checking account), and $28,273.22 (money market account).

My mom's estate was being set up for the vultures. Her life was being handed over to the highest bidder. My daughter was STILL legally her health care surrogate and my mom STILL had all her legal rights, and she had been appointed an attorney to represent her.

On May 5, 2011, through an "Order Appointing Examining Committee" signed by the probate judge, three strangers were named and appointed to examine "the alleged incapacited person." My mom did not know or have a part in choosing anyone to examine her. No one explained to my mom what the examination was for, no one gave her the option of rejecting or refusing to go into the hearing, and no one explained the consequences or possible results of the hearing. She was not given any statement informing her of her rights to choose her own doctor and have her own attorney before undergoing the exam, she was not warned it could be used against her in court to take away her civil rights and she would then become a "non person", like a child. They just forced this on her without any explanation.

On May 5, 2011, my oldest sister took my mom to see Dr. Bernie Marrero, a psychologist. Many of the statements and information provided to him regarding my mom were incorrect, including the number of siblings my mother had in her family. For example, my sister stated to Dr. Marrero,

> "that Mrs. Tozzo experiences procedural memory difficulties, primarily with the phone and remote control. In addition, she has experienced 3-4 falls within the past 3 years. In addition, Dr. Tozzo reports changes in Ms. Tozzo's personality. In the past, she was highly anxious and domineering, requiring the use of anxiolytic medications."

My mom never took anxiolytic medications under her primary care physician from 2000-2012. However, Dr. Marrero stated that my mom had "probable late onset of dementia" and "impaired memory," a diagnosis that cannot be medically determined in one visit. But he also recommended that my mom's family be seen to "discuss **the results** of the cognitive evaluation to formulate plans for caregiving assistance to comply with prescribed medications." He never stated whether or not she can make health care and financial decisions on her own or with a reliable adult's assistance. The only thing he recommended was that my mom needed "caregiving assistance" to help with nutrition, personal hygiene, and medications. Even though my daughter and I were listed as her caregivers, we were never contacted to review the results. Dr. Marrero did **not make** any recommendations for my mom to be under guardianship. He never contacted me about the results, and he never asked me about my mom's history or lifestyle.

My sister presented a "diagnosis" of my mother's condition to Dr. Marrero, which is a direct conflict of interest and unethical, in any medical profession, for anyone to diagnose a family member. Dr.

Marrero should not have accepted this information as a licensed professional.

On May 17, 2011, Ms. Brasington filed a "Petition to Determine a Hearing for Incapacity (not alleged incapacity) and to Appoint Limited and Standby Guardian." The committee had not yet met with my mother.

May 17, 2011 – "Notice of Filing Copy of Designation of Healthcare Surrogate." My oldest daughter was already the designated healthcare surrogate for my mom since October 2007, and my mom had not yet been deemed "incapacitated." A copy of my mom's living will/designation of health care surrogate was sent to my attorney on April 26, 2011, who forwarded the document to Attorney Brasington. According to the Notice of May 17, 2011, Ms. Brasington states that "the attached copy of Designation of Healthcare Surrogate which, the Court should note, does not contain any provisions containing a waiver of Carmen Tozzo's HIPPA rights under federal law to the named health care representative" and "which is not a reasonably less restrictive alternative to guardianship that will sufficiently and adequately protect Carmen Tozzo." The only thing missing from the 2007 document designating a health care surrogate was the permission for my daughter to have access to my mom's medical records, which could have been very easily revised by a judge, since my mom had not yet been seen by the Examining Committee.

So appointing a guardian, a stranger, who my mom did not know and want, was "a reasonably less restrictive alternative"?

Mind boggling.

However, the November 7, 2011 "Order Appointing Guardian of Person and Property" states that Marilyn Belo, the first plenary guardian, has the right to "make any medical, surgical, or treatment decisions for Carmen Tozzo" and the previously designated health care surrogate is "revoked pursuant to FS 744.3115."

FS 744.3115 states the following:

"[p]ursuant to the grounds listed in s.765.105, the court, upon its own motion, may, with <u>notice to the surrogate and any other appropriate parties</u>, modify or revoke the authority of the surrogate to make health care decisions for the ward. Any order revoking or modifying the authority of the surrogate **MUST BE SUPPORTED by specific written findings OF FACT**."

Not only was my daughter never contacted or received any notice, but there was never supportive evidence of fact presented that stated <u>why she should not make the decisions</u> for her grandmother. The plenary guardian had no medical background. My daughter was a BSN, and currently a Nurse Practitioner. Furthermore, according to **FS 706.205**, my mom's consent was never asked, and regardless of her capacity, medical procedures and side effects of medications must be explained to the patient in the presence of an authorized representative. No such consent or documentation existed in any of my mom's medical records.

On May 24, 2011, in 65 minutes (one hour and 5 minutes), the examining committee determined that my mom was an "incapacitated person." They never took Dr. Marrero's recommendation ("probably dementia or the Alzheimer's type"), or the recommendation of my mom's primary care physician for the past 12 years. I was never contacted by any of the committee members or asked any questions regarding my mom, her care, or her situation. They determined that she did not have the right to make informed decisions:

· about marriage,
· about voting,
· about applying for government benefits,
· to driving a vehicle,
· to travel,
· about the right to seek employment,

· about the right to (sign a) contract,
· to assist in the defense of suits of any nature against her,

· to manage property or make any gift of disposition of property,
· to determine her place of residents,
· regarding her right to medical/mental health treatment, and
· affecting social environment or other social aspects of her life.

The rights they took away from her in 65 minutes, were in direct violation of her:
· **1st Amendment** (Freedom of speech and religion);
· **6th Amendment** ("the right to a lawyer...the right to know who your accusers are, the nature of the charges and evidence against you");
· Direct violation of the American with Disabilities Act (ADA) of 1990, which prohibits discrimination against individuals with disabilities in all areas of public life) and,

· **14th Amendment** ("no state shall make or enforce any law which shall abridge the privileges or immunities of citizens of the U.S., now shall any state deprive any person of life, liberty, or property, without due process of law, nor deny to any person within its jurisdiction the equal protection of the law.")

There was no gerontologist on the committee, none of these individuals had ever met, previously examined, evaluated, spoken to, or knew my mom's medical history prior to May 24, 2011. My mom had the legal right to have her attorney present, but he was not at the competency hearing, which should have been grounds to have the hearing dismissed. My mom was never tested for drugs in her system, which would greatly impair her ability to respond to their questions. According to the ADA, if the questions asked of my mom at the hearing were intended to "discriminate or skew" her responses in any way, she had the right to review them prior to the hearing. I knew in my heart that my mom had been drugged going into that hearing. I had no proof, but as with other feelings that I had throughout the guardianship, they were usually spot on.

I had the same feeling about that day.

When I spent numerous days and nights with my mom prior to guardianship, I knew that she watched the news several times a day, including the morning, 6 pm and 11 pm news. She knew her current events, she knew who the president, first lady, vice-president and other U.S. government officials were. I was given very short notice regarding the hearing, and not given the option of taking my mom to the hearing.

I am not sure what that word "incapacitated" means in terms of what they were trying to accomplish or why they asked her so many benign questions that day. A person is incapacitated when they have surgery, have the flu, or recovering from any medical procedure, but legal incapacity is an entirely different matter altogether. In many jurisdictions, a Respondent in a Petition for Incapacity has the right to a jury trial. My mom received none of that.

Prior to the hearing, I contacted all three committee members, but only one contacted me **after** the hearing, Dr. Brian Cooke, and as stated on page 8 of the report, "Another of Ms. Tozzo's daughter, Teresa Lyles, Ph.D., admitted that her mother has 'some memory problems' but she stated, 'I do not believe she is demented or incapacitated.' This is not what I told him when we spoke. What I said to him was that for my mom's age, her memory was really good, but has some problems from time to time. I also told him that everyone and anyone over the age of 40 has "memory problems." He admitted, and agreed, that this was often true. When speaking with my younger sister, who drove my mom to the hearing, Dr. Cooke stated, "Elena

Clark (petitioner) stated that her mother has been having memory problems with her short-term memory for the past three years. She has had trouble with cleaning her house and with cooking, sometimes even forgetting how to use the microwave."

Not one mention of my mom having "memory problems" in the previous three years was ever noted by her primary care physicians. My mom cooked for herself all the time, including the use of her microwave. These were all inconsistencies, and false statements.

By the way, if the examining committee finds an alleged incapacitated person as having capacity, they are not paid for their evaluation. They are only paid for deeming the person "incapacitated." Their payment comes **directly** out of the incapacitated person's estate, without their knowledge or consent.

According to 744.331(3)(c);

"The Chief Judge shall prepare a list of persons qualified to be members of an examining committee as required by statute. Counsel for the Petitioner in incapacity proceedings shall select members of the examining committee from the list prepared by the Chief Judge. The examining committee fees shall be paid by the guardian from the property of the ward...."[3]

The judges, the attorney for my sisters, and the future guardian all had something to gain. My mom and I didn't stand a chance. I was never told about these dysfunctional relationships by my attorney.

On **May 27, 2011**: "Petition to Approve Monthly Budget For Expenditures" and "Petition For Order Designating Depository for Assets" were filed. The money was already being distributed. My mom was never consulted or made aware of what was going on with her finances. She was never allowed to read her own mail, especially after

---

[3]

http://circuit8.org/web/ao/7%2004%20(v3)(s)(p)%20Appt%20%20of%20Exam%2 0C'tee%20Members.pdf her move to the first lock down facility. Everything was pre-meditated, including her guardianship and her death.

Everything was planned.

Everything was about the money.

My mom would have needed home health. I would 100% agree to that. The problem was that she had money and other family members wanted to take it. They knew the close emotional and spiritual relationship my daughters and I had with my mom. They used the guardians to isolate her from the family that really cared about her, drug her with illegal chemical restraints without her knowledge, and take the money that my dad had rightfully left her.

This is what guardianship is all about. Take what you can, in the quickest time that you can, kill the ward, and move onto the next victim. It's a pattern, and it happens in every state in U.S.

Several years after my mom had been turned over to guardians and while she was still alive, I found out that the probate examining committee members are appointed by probate judges, as previously stated. The probate judges have a direct influence on these members since they appoint them. The unsuspecting victim does not know if they are family, friends or acquaintances of the judge, any local attorneys or of the guardians. It is all "seniors for cash," similar to the now famous "Kids for Cash" scheme in Pennsylvania."[4]

The Kids for Cash scheme, which came to light in 2008, involved Luzerne County Court Judges Mark Ciavarella and Senior Judge Michael Counaham. Both were convicted of accepting money from Robert Mericle, the builder of two private, for-profit, youth centers for juveniles. The judges conspired to build a new juvenile delinquent facility and then stock it with children in exchange for a $1 million investment and then dividend payments when each child was

---

4

http://www.mintpressnews.com/judge-sentenced-to-28-years-for-selling-kids-for-cash-to-prisons/209013/ number of juveniles per year. You can also cite to the movie, "Kids for Cash" now on Net housed. They even went so far as to sign a statement with the bank guaranteeing placement of a minimum number of juveniles per year. The documentary, "Kids for Cash" is now on Netflix.

The three strangers on the examining committee were paid **$1,200.00** ($20 per minute) out of my mom's bank account to deem her incapacitated. My mom paid three strangers to deem her incapacitated, at the hands of my sisters, an attorney and a probate judge who signed all the orders.

My mom did not want to be at the capacity hearing.

My mom did not have her attorney present at the hearing, a cause for <u>dismissal</u> of the proceedings.

My mom did not even know where she was going or why she was there.

My mom did not want to leave her home or be under guardianship.

Three strangers decided her fate on that morning of May 24, 2011 in **65 minutes**. This was the first step to her death sentence.

My mom was taken from her home to the first lock down on May 25, 2012. She was in fairly good health for a 93 year old woman. She was mobile, did not use a walker, she was active, she traveled, she went to numerous social events, and she was cognitively aware. I took her to church almost every Sunday without fail. She slept at my house on many weekends. She enjoyed the outdoors and going shopping. Dozens of friends and family socialized, and interacted, with her.

My mom died on May 24, 2015, three years after being taken from her home on May 25, 2012. At the time of her death, at 96, my mom was completely confined to a wheel chair, she had been isolated from her family, friends and not allowed to attend church for at least two years. She had not attended a family function with me in four years. She was not allowed out of the facility for meals. The falls, including multiple head injuries my mom experienced, along with the massive doses of drugs and chemical restraint orders, caused my mom to develop several very noticeable conditions. My mom began having jerky movements when she walked and tried to hold objects like a cup or utensil. Sometimes, she couldn't complete sentences, and would stumble on her words. My mom was in Stage III renal failure and developed Chronic Obstructive Pulmonary Disease (COPD) under guardianship. My mom also had some lapses in memory under guardianship, where she thought she was in a different era than the present. For example, even though my dad had died in 1999, she would say, "he died about 10 years, ago, right?" However, I would remind her that we were in 2014, or 2015, and that it was 15 or 16 years since he had died. It wasn't until the third or fourth time this happened that I realized that her memory after guardianship, and when the drugging started, was about the same time that her "time lines" began to be a little off.

She would always be fairly on target with my children's ages. She always recognized them, and my friends who visited her at the lock down facilities. She knew who the guardians were, and we had code names for them, because we would always say, "the walls have ears." Despite everything they did to her, she continued to love and be happy during our visits, and sad when I would leave. She would always hold my hand tight and ask me to sleep with her.

They didn't think she would last three years. My mom was that strong. I was that determined.

According to the Florida Bar, "any adult resident, related or unrelated to the potential ward, of Florida can serve as a guardian,"[5] and may file a petition with the court to determine another person's incapacity. It does not matter if they know the person or not. From that point, it is easy to hand that elder over to the courts. This is stated on numerous attorney and guardian web sites.

Any person over the age of 18 can be a guardian. The **ONLY** requirement in Florida to be a professional guardian is to take a 40 hour course, which costs approximately $400. Some states prefer

---

[5]http://www.floridabar.org/tfb/TFBConsum.nsf/48e76203493b82ad85256 7090070c9b9/e8fd739d221b11c085256b2f006c5a4e

family members over non family and especially those family members that can take the disabled person home and care for them there.

All guardians in Florida must abide by Florida Statute (FS) 744, which determines what the legal guidelines are for every guardian. Not only do the guardians not abide by FS 744, but the judges and their attorneys ignore it as well.

More Smoke Screens

Meanwhile, my aunt was still being held in rehab April and May 2011. I did not understand why she had to be there for so long. It was already more than 1 ½ months that she had been there. She was miserable and wasn't eating. I tried to bring her the food that she loved. In the early morning of May 9, 2011, I received a call from the facility doctor. He let me know that my aunt was severely anemic and had to be hospitalized for a transfusion. He told me that she could have gone home weeks earlier, but he would only release her after the transfusion. I began to make arrangements for my aunt to come home. This is the typical revolving door of facility to hospital and then back again because they plop down a tray for a half hour and don't make sure the patients eat or drink sufficiently. It can often be contrived so that when the hospitals need to fill beds they let the nursing homes know, and when the nursing homes need to fill beds, they let the hospitals know. One hand washes the other and in the meantime, elders and disabled's are abused by fake malnutrition and dehydration which only takes a day or two to occur. Once in the hospital, to keep a patient in a bed, often fake procedures are ordered. For example, sitting a group of Alzheimer's disease patients in front of a television watching a movie and billing for "group therapy."[6] The workers know about this but can't report the abuse because the licensing agencies will attack their licenses and often blackball them.

On May 13, 2011, I arrived at the rehab facility and fought to bring my aunt home. I was aggressively stopped by the facility social

---

[6] http://www.acfe.com/article.aspx?id=4294976280

worker, who had already made a pact with my sisters to keep my aunt at the facility. My aunt was prevented from leaving her room, until she demanded to go home. She was competent, after all, and they could not hold her there against her will.

My older sister had taken my aunt's house key, but my mom and I were able to call a locksmith to change the lock. When she arrived home that day, my aunt's refrigerator had old and molding food, and roach droppings were everywhere. An exterminator had to be called, and the refrigerator had to be cleaned out. My mom and I had enlisted a home health agency, and my aunt now had 24-hour care. She was happy to be home. Her first meal, which I bought, was Cuban food and coffee. I spent the last $30 I had to my name on food for my mom, aunt and two children.

Someone contacted DCF the day I brought my aunt home on May 13th. This was the second call to DCF. The claim was that I had removed my aunt "to take advantage of her, and that I had taken over $40,000 from my mom." I didn't even have to go in for an interview to the DCF office for this second accusation. I emailed the agent and stated that my older sister had confiscated all my aunt's identification, credit cards, checkbook, Medicare card, and picture identification. I was never contacted again by this agent. The investigation was closed on May 19, 2011. No one did anything to these people who were 'breaking the law' but allowed an innocent person to be accused – that would be me.

There was one more call to DCF on August 15, 2011.

CHAPTER 4
THE Guardianship Begins

FS 744.1012 Legislative intent.—The Legislature finds that adjudicating a person totally incapacitated and in need of a guardian deprives such person of all her or his civil and legal rights and that such deprivation may be unnecessary. The Legislature further finds that it is desirable to make available the least restrictive form of guardianship to assist persons who are only partially incapable of caring for their needs. Recognizing that every individual has unique needs and differing abilities, <u>the Legislature declares that it is the purpose of this act to promote the public welfare by establishing a system that permits incapacitated persons to participate as fully as possible in all decisions affecting them;</u> that assists such persons in meeting the essential requirements for their physical health and safety, in protecting their rights, in managing their financial resources, and in **<u>developing or regaining their abilities to the maximum extent possible</u>**; and that accomplishes these objectives through providing, in each case, the form of assistance that least interferes with the legal capacity of a person to act in her or his own behalf. This act shall be liberally construed to accomplish this purpose.

In total, **more than 460 documents** were filed between April 29, 2011 and April 4, 2016, with four guardians (one emergency and three plenary), their attorneys, and three of my own attorneys. I received less than 20% of these legal documents from my attorneys and/or guardians' or the guardians' attorneys.

The guardians and their attorneys were paid in excess of $100,000.00 that I can determine – I was never given access to my mom's finances or a final accounting. My mom was never given access to her own finances. My mom never knew what they were spending. They took away my dad's pension, his social security, and veteran's benefits. They kept my mom in unsafe facilities, as she was neglected and abused.

Hundreds of these documents were filed by the first plenary guardian. Oftentimes, she filed them several times due to errors, or filed the same petition numerous times. For example, the first plenary guardian filed four different petitions to open my mom's safety deposit box, signed and unsigned documents – twice on December 29, 2011, and twice on January 17, 2012. Numerous motions and petitions were frivolous and had no legal bearing or merit to the guardianship or my mother's care, well-being and in her best interest. For almost every time the first guardian requested monetary compensation from the courts, including the permission to sell my mom's home, my sisters filed petitions of 'no objection' to the charges.

It has always been my understanding that the guardianship accounting is closed to the family and the ward. An interested party has to file an injunction to view the documents, but only if the probate judge allows it. I never agreed to anything. Only one of my attorneys protested one of the expenses, which was the sale of my mom's house. After the sham of the competency hearing, another hearing was then set for an emergency guardian. My sisters had petitioned to be a limited guardian and back-up guardian, but I petitioned to be my mom's permanent guardian, which took precedence over both a limited and back-up guardian. My sisters had hired a local attorney, who ended up also being the attorney for the first emergency guardian. This emergency guardian had also known my younger sister, on a personal and professional basis, for many years. This conflict of interest was never reported to my attorney or the courts.

It is the attorney's obligation to recuse themselves because of the conflict of interest. This is what SHOULD happen. According to the Florida Bar "the court may not appoint a guardian in some circumstances in which a conflict of interest may occur"[7]. It would not have made a difference to any of the probate judges. The law and my mom's rights did not matter to them.

Money talks, and bullshit walks, as the saying goes.

The first hearing on June 2, 2011 started with a barrage of accusations against me, primarily that I had stolen money from my mom. Remember, DCF had already been contacted. I had been investigated and I was cleared of any and all accusations. The hearing had to be stopped and postponed because the opposing attorney (Brasington) had not given my attorney all the documentation she was using against me in court. The second hearing was in September 2, 2011. I wish I had known then what I know now about guardianship. The accusations against me were a **smoke screen**. These accusations, which continued even after my mom's death, were only a diversion so that they could isolate, medicate, and drain my mom's estate.

A lot happened between June and September 2011, including the third, and last, DCF call against me.

The courts appointed Bonnie DiVito as the first emergency guardian on June 6, 2011. She did not disclose her relationship to my sister, and did not disclose the name of her attorney to the courts, or to my attorney. The document acknowledged that they had "executed an advanced directive," but the emergency guardian "shall exercise authority over any health care surrogate until further order of this Court," which never happened. Again, my daughter was never notified of a hearing and there was no factual testimony or documentation

---

[7]

http://www.floridabar.org/tfb/TFBConsum.nsf/48e76203493b82ad85256709007 0c9b9/e8fd739d221b11c085256b2f006c5a4e.

stating why the directives should not be followed. This was a due process violation under the 5th Amendment.

The holder of a Power of Attorney or any advance directives, has the right to notice, a petition describing the cause of action against a Respondent, discovery, a briefing schedule and a trial, preferably a jury trial. After the first DCF charge, in addition to taking care of my sick daughter and an another, under aged daughter, working, checking on my mom and disabled aunt (now home and wheelchair bound with 24-hour care), I also had to hire back-up care for my mom when I couldn't stay with her. Other than my daughters, no other family member helped caregiving, with scheduling the caregivers, and to make sure the sitters (agency and non-agency) were paid. If I miscalculated hours, I had to cover those hours, which meant either bringing my mom home with me or staying with her in her home with her. I was never paid for being a private caregiver or any of the supplies and food that I provided for her under guardianship. The discord and arguments between my sisters and I escalated. My oldest daughter, the designated and legal health care surrogate for both my mom and aunt, was never consulted or allowed to make any decisions for either of them during this time – during guardianship and time of illness. Family caretakers are generally not paid and there will be no kickbacks received from a family member. However, a nursing home provides campaign donations to the judges and kickbacks to the GAL's, the probate attorneys and others who have court influence to place them in a nursing home. So family never gets paid and never is preferred, while nursing home placement is either a goal or assured.

Again, one hand washes the other in this game of greed and evil.

Despite the stressful circumstances, the nights I spent with my mom, and visiting my aunt was priceless. I felt guilty about leaving my children at home, but I had to make some difficult choices at the time. I was torn, because I knew they all needed me. But I felt my mom needed me most. No one else was protecting her. I could not be in two places at once, and I needed to keep an eye on what was going on with my mom.

Every time I spent the night, my mom and I would visit my aunt and watch TV with her until bedtime. Usually, I was the one falling asleep on my aunt's couch. I was that exhausted that I would pass out before these two elderly ladies. We all held hands and kissed and hugged during that time. I treasure these moments and everything they said to me. My mom and I would eat together, watch the evening news and her programs, and then talk about family and children. We always prayed, and then it was bedtime. I tucked her in, we hugged and kissed. This was our routine, one that would soon end permanently. I was always mindful and alert if she needed help to the bathroom during the night, but for the most part, she either stayed in bed until early morning or went to the bathroom on her own. I made coffee and breakfast for her each morning. She liked to stay in her pajamas for a little while. She felt comfortable that way. I waited until the caregiver came, then said goodbye until that evening or the next day.

We grew closer, if that was possible, and she began to heal my heart, slowly but surely. I didn't understand what was happening then, or that it was actually happening, but she was my spiritual guide and my angel. We never imagined that things would get worse, and what we would all have to go through in the coming years.

My mom had lost a kidney due to stones and other complications when she was 66. My oldest daughter was only about 18 months at the time, and my parents were still living in Miami. She lived a very healthy life, and made excellent food choices after her kidney operation – no salt, low fat foods, and little to no sweets.[8] I noticed

---
8

It should be noted here that table salt, or NaCl is toxic to the human body and is about 1/3 a crystalline structure like glass that irritates and scrapes or irritates the insides of the veins and arteries and that is why it is best to use sea salt, which is essential to the body because the body lives on micro electronic signals which are communicated only by salt. Sugar is highly toxic

when my mom was in her late 80s that she was having trouble with holding her bladder. As a mother of three daughters, and now having experienced some bladder issues myself, I understand that this is not unusual at this age, or any age after 50 for that matter. I had no problem doing her laundry and changing her sheets if they were soiled. It was my pleasure to help her. She was a bit embarrassed, but I played it off as not being a big deal. After all, wasn't this the same woman who had cleaned my poop, pee and vomit for many years when I was a child? It was my duty as her daughter to help her with these transitions as she aged. She thanked me, but I always thanked her instead for taking such good care of me as a child, and taking care of, and loving, my three daughters.

Other family members immediately tried to push adult diapers on her, but she resisted the change and she got angry. It was about giving up her independence. For me, it was about being kind and loving to my mom about these sensitive and life changing issues. Instead, I talked her into a bed pad, and she agreed. It wasn't until she entered the first lock down facility that they forced my mom to use adult diapers full time. I guess it's a requirement since the residents there were on bathroom schedules. My mom was often locked out of her room to access her bathroom. She had dozens of UTI's, an infection that if left untreated, causes delirium in elderly people.[9]

While still under the temporary emergency guardian, and one night that I was at my mom's house, my older sister and her boyfriend showed up on August 10, 2011. It was dark outside and we had already turned off my mom's porch light. The encounter escalated to verbal abuse, and also to where the boyfriend threatened me, and then

---

to the human body and should be avoided. Carbs turn quickly into sugar and they[9] should also be avoided.

UTI's are often eliminated with good supplementation of lypospheric or Lyposomal vitamin C, 3-6 gr. per day, and probiotics (Florajen, PB8, Mercola). Good hydration and emptying the bladder as soon as full or near full are also are essential.

eventually grabbed my mom's arm, leaving a bruise. Under Florida Statute (FS) 784, this is considered assault and battery on a vulnerable person. I called 9-11 twice that night – once when the screaming began and he threatened me, and the second time after he grabbed my mom. The police officer refused to arrest him because my sister corroborated his story, despite the fact that he admitted grabbing my mom and it is noted in the police report. Both told the officer that my mom had Alzheimer's disease. My mom was not diagnosed with this illness. Very clearly and succinctly, my mom explained to the male officer what had happened and then asked for the EMTs. She told the four male EMTs the same story. I had never felt so threatened and horrified at what I witnessed that night. I could barely sleep. I slept in bed with my mom that night. We held each other and prayed. I didn't think it could get worse. I was wrong. The next day, I contacted the emergency guardian and explained the events of the previous night. My sister was told that her boyfriend was not allowed in my mom's house.

On August 15, 2011, I was contacted by DCF for the third time. The accusation this last time was that I "was rough with (my mom) and left bruises on her" and that I "had also taken a large sum of money." I had already been cleared of the "stealing money" accusation two months earlier by DCF. When I entered the DCF office this last time, the same agent, who had been the first investigative agent, was incredibly annoyed and apologetic. He understood that what had happened was a personal attack.

According to the Florida Department of Children and Families[10], "any person who **knowingly and willfully makes a false report** or counsels another to make a false report is guilty of a **felony of the third degree** punishable by up to five years in prison. In addition, the department may impose a fine not to exceed $10,000 for

---

[10]

http://www.myflfamilies.com/service-programs/abuse-hotline/false-reportingguidelines

each violation. Each time that a false report is made constitutes a separate violation. A false report is a report of child abuse, neglect or abandonment, or adult abuse, neglect or exploitation that is made to the central abuse hotline which is not true and is maliciously made for the purpose of:

· Harassing, embarrassing, or harming another person;
· Personal financial gain for the reporting person;
· Acquiring custody of a child or vulnerable adult; or

· Personal benefit for the reporting person in any other private dispute involving a child or vulnerable adult.

Section 415.111, F.S. addresses false reporting for adults.

Three false reports were filed against me. DCF is obligated to report and pursue those who make fraudulent report, of which they never did. The third investigation was closed on September 6, 2011 stating that "there is no credible evidence to support the allegations of Physical Injury and Exploitation."

I was never contacted by DCF again. But there was more abuse and harassment to come.

About two weeks later, during Labor Day weekend, my children and I had planned a cook out with my mom and aunt. I had emailed the guardian in advance of my plans. My youngest daughter and I arrived first at my mom's house. When I entered my mom's home on September 5, 2011, I saw my sister, her boyfriend and youngest son sitting near my mom. I asked him to leave as per the guardian's orders, but he refused. I went outside, called the guardian first, and when I could not reach her, I called the police. The female police officer heard him cursing and making an obscene gesture at my 16-year-old daughter. My sister and her boyfriend attempted the same story from two weeks prior – that my mom had Alzheimer's. This time, the officer asked my mom what she wanted to do, and my mom very clearly stated that she did not want the man in her house. He was issued a "no trespass" order and asked to never come onto my mom's property again.

During the following weeks after this Labor Day incident, my older sister took my mom out for dinner multiple times. No caregiver was ever with her. Remember, the examining committee had stated that my mom "did not have the capacity affecting social environment or other social aspects of her life." When my mom arrived at the restaurant, the boyfriend was sitting at the table waiting. My mom called me after the first incident in a very agitated state. She told me what happened. I complained to the guardian, but she refused to protect my mother.

On September 29, 2011, my aunt passed away in her bed at home. During the last month of her life, her health had slowly begun to decline. I was lying next to her and she was in my arms as she passed. Her paid attendant/caregiver was also present. I contacted the hospice nurse, and she and the owner of the home health agency arrived within 15 minutes. He had contacted both my siblings, but I vehemently stated that **only family** was allowed in the home. My sister arrived about 15 minutes later with her boyfriend. I asked him to stay outside while my sister came inside to pay her respects. He called the police and in the police report, it was stated that I was "an unruly person" and that I had "assaulted him."

This time I had three witnesses to corroborate my story.

My three daughters had arrived and gone to my mom's house to be with, and comfort, her. My two oldest daughters were at my side when the sheriff's deputies arrived at my aunt's home. I stayed until almost 11 pm when they took my aunt's body to the funeral home.

The following day, I was advised by the emergency guardian that I could no longer spend nights with my mom. All caregivers that I had hired were dismissed without a reason. A new agency was hired. One of many decisions that was self-serving to the guardians and not in my mom's best interest. I asked her to reconsider in an email for my mom's best interest.

On October 6, 2011, I asked the temporary guardian to protect my mom and not make any changes to her caregivers. I told her that my sister's boyfriend was "unstable, and I have already had 2 separate police officers ask me why my mom's guardian isn't protecting her."

She stated, "The incidents with you or your daughters cannot justify a restraining order on your Mother and we cannot control Mr. Clark's whereabouts." She continues to state that the reason the caregivers were removed was because "when a caregiver does not understand who gives the orders they need to go." But also said that "your mom said she was OK and had nothing against her" (them).

My mom was extremely saddened and blue after my aunt died, which was natural because she had just lost her last sibling, as well as her best friend. With that being said, my mom was never diagnosed with any psychological disorder. My aunt's funeral was extremely strained.

About a year later, in August 21 2012, and after my sister and her boyfriend had already broken up, I heard he was found dead in his home. There were rumors that his death came under very suspicious circumstances but I cannot confirm this story, only that he died.

The Worst Is Yet To Come - Isolation

The second, and final, probate hearing for guardianship was in early September 2011. After the June 2011 hearing, my mom was never again allowed to go to or defend herself in court, which is her constitutional right. I know she wanted to go because she asked me multiple times. The guardians refused to take her to any court hearings. She also asked me to hire an attorney when she was taken from her home the following year and put in the first lock down. I was fighting to see my mom, and tried to hire an attorney for her, but the guardians used all her money to fight me.

At this hearing, and in front of the first probate judge, my attorney disclosed several conflicts of interest between my sisters', their attorney, and the emergency guardian. There was no recusal by the attorney who represented my sisters and the guardian. My mom's appointed attorney was present at this hearing. From my recollection of that day, my mom's attorney stated to the judge that <u>he felt my mom was competent and did not need a guardian</u>. After her appointment in November, 2011, the first plenary guardian did not allow my mother to keep her attorney. My attorney also argued that since I had applied for permanent guardianship, there was nothing prohibiting me from taking this role. None of this made any difference to the judge that day, and he proceeded to ask the emergency guardian "her opinion," even though the judge had just heard her admit to the conflict of interest. She recommended a stranger for permanent guardianship to handle my mom's life. Marilyn Cangro Belo was appointed.

They were nailing the coffin shut.

Prior to the appointment of the first plenary guardian in November 2011, my attorney recommended mediation between my sisters and I, but they refused then, and on at least one other occasion. I sent several emails to my sisters, prior to June 2011, making attempts to include a third party mediator, a pastor, or someone else. All attempts were ignored or refused.

After her appointment, I met with the first plenary guardian on November 17, 2011 for the first time. I had never met her prior to that day. The first words out of her mouth were "I'm going to put your mom in a facility." Since this was totally against my mother's wishes, I thought she needed some persuasion. My oldest daughter and I sent emails begging to allow my mother to live with either of us. In my email, I told the guardian that I would sign any legal documents to hand over my inheritance to my siblings.

I stated:

"Finally, the issue with my mom's finances and her future. I expressed that if my mom goes to an assisted living/nursing home, she will more than likely not last there for very long…She will die there of a broken heart. I know that you said you would not have her move in with me, but I am asking you to reconsider. I will work 2 or 3 jobs to help support my mom, and I will even pay for the private security guards to be at my home if my sisters want time with her, as well as me leaving during that time when they are there. Sell her house, give whatever money my sisters want and let me take care of my mom. That is all I want. I don't want anything else, only to care for her…My 3 children and I took care of my mom for about 2 years. My daughters and I also feel the same way, and we feel very strongly about this. I will do whatever it takes to allow my sisters their time with her…please just think this over carefully, as my mom's quality of life is #1. My mom is happiest when she is surrounded by her family. She is all about FAMILY."

My oldest daughter did the same in a similar email – pleading not to remove my mom from her home.

She refused to hear our side.

The Harassment Begins – The First Thanksgiving and Christmas Under Guardianship

I had been given "permission" to have my mom over for Thanksgiving (2011), which had been pre-approved by the first temporary guardian. But on the Tuesday before Thanksgiving, I received an email from the guardian stating that there had "been comments made in your mother's home and to those who care for her who were concerned" that my electricity would be disconnected. She demanded a copy of a cancelled check to indicate that I had paid my electric bill or my mother would not be "allowed" to come home with me.

Another smokescreen…she was trying to get access to my bank account information.

I sent her a confirmation email of my most recent payment, and confirmed with the electric company that the electricity would not be shut off on Thanksgiving Day. I started requesting passwords on all my accounts after that day.

Wednesday, November 23, 2011 was the last night my mom spent at my house.

After that, I was never allowed to take her out for another holiday, another family birthday, graduation or special event except my daughter's wedding, or the demands were so restrictive that I refused to impose that stress on my family and mom. Without knowing what the future would hold, I spent the most amazing night with my mom. I think about these times now, and all the other nights spent with her in her home. That night on November 23, 2011, we talked, folded clothes, I made her dinner, and prepared for our last Thanksgiving with family the next day. That night, as with any night with her, was peaceful.

I had also been given "permission" to take my mom over my daughter's house to celebrate Christmas the following month. However, things turned from bad to ugly very quickly.

After firing all the caregivers that I had hired for my mom, the caregivers for the new agency began their duty in October 2011. One of the caregivers had worked with the agency that I had previously hired to care for my mom. She had been fired from this agency because she had lied to them, and me, about who she was working for. She had violated the terms of her contract with her previous employer, and was now working as an "independent" for my mom under the first Plenary Guardian. I thought this odd and called the former agency. Evidently, she was not allowed to care for my mom unless she paid a lump sum to "buy out" her former contract. In addition, she was very verbally abusive to my mom and fed my mom food that made her sick. I complained to the guardian, who was also contacted by the former agency where this caregiver worked. I received an email from the guardian stating that I was not allowed to take my mom out for Christmas because I had interfered, but my siblings were allowed to have my mom at their home for Christmas.

My family in Miami and I were sent two very disturbing Christmas cards that depicted harassing and threatening comments. We believed they were sent by my sister's boyfriend. They were signed "The Mexican," a name my sister's boyfriend had given himself the night he was at my mom's house and grabbed her arm. My Christmas card had a picture of crack pipe on it, next to the picture of baby Jesus. This is the person I had warned the emergency guardian as being unstable, and she ignored me.

After hearing the changes, my two oldest daughters drove to the guardian's office and tried to speak with her. The guardian locked herself in her office, and called the police to have my children removed from the premises. Shortly thereafter, she filed a motion to injunction – to get a restraining order against my two daughters so that they would not be able to see their grandmother. The petition was eventually dropped. She went to court to accuse my daughters, but never met or had spoken to my children. On January 27, 2012, she filed a "Notice of Voluntary Dismissal of Complaint for Injunction Relief Without Prejudice." This was an indication of things to come.

Almost immediately after the New Year (2012), I heard from several of my mom's caregivers that the guardian was looking at Assisted Living Facility facilities for my mom. My mom kept telling everyone she wanted to stay in her home – family, friends, and church members. I even tried to be a part of the process, but she refused.

On **January 11, 2012,** the guardian sent an email stating that "as of this week, January 13, 2012, there will be no visiting on Friday after 3 pm. There is no informal visits, meaning you may not drop by to see (her)" my mom.

On **January 12, 2012**, the guardian's assistant copied me on an email stating that she was refusing my visits to my mom's house and that she would try to contact "the school board," which was an attempt to gather information on my 16 year old daughter.

On **January 14, 2012,** I received an email from the guardian stating that,

> "effective January 23, unless there is a specific reason or there is a history of fully utilizing prolonged blocks of time these will not be allowed…a <u>block has been placed on the phone, the Hernandez family</u> may not contact your mother. If she wants to speak with them or their children, <u>that call will take place in my presence only</u>. If anyone attempts to remove or blocks or in any way facilitate contact with them further, steps will be taken against any offending party. If disturbing phone calls continue, other blocks will be placed or other measures taken."

The Hernandez family included my mom's nephew (my cousin), his wife, their children and grandchildren. At that time, my mom's nephew and his wife were nearly 80 years old. My mom and her nephew were more like brother and sister as they had been raised in the same home. They could not speak to her other than through my cell phone. I continued to keep vigilant about what was happening to my mom. I was kept totally in the dark about everything they were doing to her.

The guardian also changed the locks on my mom's home. I was not given a copy of the key. My mom had now been isolated from family, friends, her church, and prayer groups.

On **January 15, 2012,** I sent an email to the guardian asking her to please include me in visiting the facilities, because I wanted the same right as she was allowing my sisters. Her response was:

"I owe you no obligation to report on anything I do to whom I speak, where I go. Any communications are on a courtesy basis and they will continue in that manner."

All these actions were done <u>without a court order</u> or amendment to the existing court order.

On **February 7, 2012**, the probate judge approved an "Order to Designate Depository for Assets." In this order, the plenary guardian listed several banks where my mom held her accounts, including Wells Fargo and Florida Credit Union. The Florida Credit Union account was closed in 2012, but no record of permission to close, or accounting of assets, was ever included in any court records. They really didn't waste any time.

On **February 13, 2012**, the guardian filed a "Petition For Authorization to Sell Ward's Residence" in which she claimed that it was:

"in the best interest of the ward" and "placement in an assisted living facility would be a <u>more economic option</u> to provide the ward with necessary professional level of care in a safe environment," and also claimed that my mom's monthly expenses would exceed $11,000."

Another false document.

Another smoke screen.

Also on **February 13, 2012**, the guardian filed an "Amended Petition for Authorization to Place Ward in Assisted Living Facility." The claims in this document included that at the:

"advise of the Ward's attending physician Ward would benefit from social interaction," and "in the <u>opinion of the Guardian</u> no other safe, socially adequate or economically feasible residential placement alternative

is available to the ward at this time," and "Brookdale
Senior Living, Sterling House and Caring Bridge facility
in Gainesville Florida is a safe environment."

My mom was <u>never</u> taken to Brookdale. She was taken to
Harbor Chase, and she was placed in a lock down where
"socialization" included interactions with severely mentally ill
individuals, infrequent visits outside for fresh air, and isolation. My
mom did not have the stimulation or independence she did in her
home. The guardian never changed the court order. Numerous people
had offered to care for my mom in their home, including myself, but
the guardian refused to listen to what was in my mom's best interest.
As I will discuss later, in the so-called "safe" environments where the
guardians placed my mom, she fell almost 30 times, with many of
these falls resulting in head injuries. Under the first guardian, my mom
fell and was hospitalized 20 times. From 1999 to 2012, before she was
placed in the first lock down, my mom was never hospitalized. She was
under my care.

The **Wedding**

My oldest daughter was getting married. What a blessed
event!!! There were so many things to be grateful for in our lives. My
mom was "allowed" to help her pick out the wedding dress at the end
of January 2012. My mom attended the bridal shower on **March 17,
2012,** but at the last minute, the guardian demanded that a caregiver
accompany her. I should have recognized the red flag.

I was given "permission" to take my mom to my daughter's
wedding by myself. No restrictions. I had taken my mom on dozens of
trips to Miami, shopping, weekends to my house, and elsewhere. The
wedding was on April 7th and it was out of town in Anna Maria Island.
The week before the wedding, the guardian petitioned the courts to
have paid attendants stay with my mom at the wedding. I only agreed,
as had my daughter, to have them stay with my mom when I walked

my daughter down the aisle, took pictures and briefly during the reception, and at no other time during the weekend.

Because my daughter was a nurse, there were more than 40 professional licensed and degreed health care workers at the wedding (nurse practitioners, nurses, physical therapists, social workers), and other family members who were willing to watch my mom when I was pulled away. The guardian refused the free care and decided to pay unqualified attendants.

The guardian paid the attendants thousands of dollars out of my mother's money. My mom did not want these attendants. She wanted to be around her daughter, granddaughter and her family. About half a dozen guests that were attending the wedding sent emails to my attorney stating that they would be more than happy to help me care for my mother when needed. These emails were also forwarded to the guardian, but she refused. These paid attendants were far less qualified than the professional health care workers attending the wedding. During the week following the court hearing, and prior to my daughter's wedding, what morphed from agreeing to have one attendant at the wedding for a few hours, turned into the demand by the guardian to have an attendant by my mom's side <u>the entire weekend</u>, including at the rehearsal dinner, and <u>sitting outside the room at the house where my mom and I slept</u>. However, the day prior to the wedding, I picked my mom up at 8 am, and we arrived at about

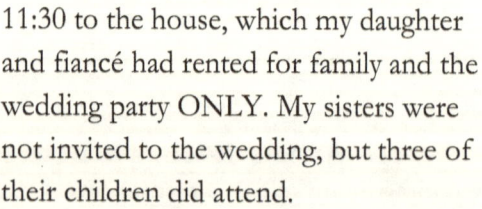

11:30 to the house, which my daughter and fiancé had rented for family and the wedding party ONLY. My sisters were not invited to the wedding, but three of their children did attend.

On **March 6, 2012**, I had sent the guardian the location of the house where we were staying. On March 22nd, I gave her the time when I would pick up my mom (April 6th, 8 am). The night prior to leaving for the wedding (April 5 at 9:48 pm), the harassment began. The guardian sent my attorney and I an email stating,

> "if I do not have the address of the place Mrs. Tozzo will be staying while out of town, I will <u>report to the court</u> on Monday that Ms. Lyles defied the court's order and obstructed my work as guardian."

I resent the email I had originally sent from March 6th. The guardian was just getting started and the harassment had just begun.

At **4:59 pm on April 6**[th], the guardian sent an email to my attorney and me stating:

> "the young woman from Nursecore is at the Bradenton Beach address now, <u>she arrived at **5:00**</u> and I have asked her to call me at **5:45** with an update. If no one is at the location I will assume this is rejection of service <u>and file accordingly with the court</u>."

At <u>5:29 pm</u>, I texted my attorney, "we are all here sitting at the restaurant. Don't see caregiver."

At <u>8:19 pm</u>, the guardian sent another text to me and my attorney, "if you do not do as you agreed and court requires I will call <u>DCF</u> and report elder abuse. You told us you wanted your mother and we agreed. Is there something going on at the house that people should know about. Maybe I should give the address now to the police, it seems you need help. Your mother best be at that house tom (Sic), I am making arrangements for her to be brought to gville (Sic) she can see pictures of the wedding."

After this verbal abuse and harassment continued for another hour or so, I finally asked the guardian to rent my mom and I a hotel room away from the wedding party, or come pick up my mom, and drive her back to Gainesville. The disruptions were stressing everyone, including my mom, and especially my daughter, the bride. The guardian rented a room, but requested from both the hotel manager and the caregiver, a stranger my mom and I had never met, to not

allow me to spend the night with my mom.

Incidentally, the <u>court order</u> requiring home health to accompany my mom outside of her home was not signed until **April 10, 2012, three days AFTER** my daughter's wedding.

Fortunately, the wedding was beautiful, but I missed watching my three daughters get dressed, getting their hair and make-up done, and many picture opportunities. My mom had an amazing time. She cried when my daughter got married, and marveled at the beautiful day, especially the crystal clear water of the beach. My mom loved the beach, and that is where my daughter was married, with sand between everyone's toes, and the smell of salt water in the air. It was truly a magical day.This would be the only grandchild's wedding that my mom would attend. We cherish this event with all our hearts, with memories and pictures. We spoke about it often when she was still alive. She remembered every detail of that day. I was by her side every moment, except when she was sleeping, only because I was restricted. She begged me to stay with her each night, but I was there early in the morning, despite only sleeping just a few hours each night.

On the day of the wedding, I had instructed the paid attendant, who was going to bring my mom to the location, to drop my mom off <u>at the door</u> of the reception so my mom did not have to walk, but instead of following my directions, she parked several blocks away and made my mom walk. My mom's feet and ankles were swollen by the time she got there. The attendant had also forgotten to bring an extra adult diaper, and my mom's night medications. She also ate the food that she was not supposed to eat, and paid for by my daughter.

My mom danced at that wedding. She danced with the bride, with me, her nephew, and five other grandchildren. She ate, laughed, sat with her family from Miami, took pictures, and enjoyed the beautiful day. At about 11 pm, I drove my mom back to her hotel. She didn't want to leave the party. My mom was so happy. The next day, we drove home. We talked about the wedding and how wonderful it was to see her oldest grandchild get married. She never forgot that day.

On **April 10, 2012** the probate judge approved an "Order Establishing Permanent Visitation Schedule" and an "Order Authorizing Sale of Ward's Residence." The guardian stated:

"family members have regularly imposed on the scheduled visits of the other family members resulting in distress to the ward and exacerbating family disharmony;

the court ordered visitation schedule applies to each of the ward's three daughters only. All other family members....must request <u>permission</u> for a scheduled visiting time directly from the Plenary Guardian...;

<u>No phone calls</u> into the ward's place of residence or from the ward's place of residence are permitted during any of the scheduled visiting times;

Infractions by any person of the visiting plan herein presented are to be reported immediately to the court for further action including but not limited to **termination of all personal visits with the ward and or incarceration**."

My sisters came and went as they pleased, but my daughters and I were constantly scrutinized and harassed by the staff of the first lock down. My mom's other family and friends were never allowed to call or see her.

CHAPTER 5 – Isolation and Medication

With the wedding behind us, and the joy of knowing that my mom had a great time, despite all the issues, I continued to visit during my designated times, even though my days and times were bumped at the guardian's whim. We were told that we had to request days/times in advance. There was no court order restricting our visits....yet.

In early morning of May 2012, I arrived to visit my mom. The second I walked into her house, I knew there was something wrong. My mom was usually very happy and excited every time I came to visit her. She would jump up from the couch or chair and fall into my arms. Today, however, I noticed a change in her. She was much more subdued today, even though I still got a hug and kiss from her. I walked down the hallway to the bathroom and discovered the source of her mood. My mom's bed, the one where she had slept in with my dad for many years, had been removed from her room, stripped of the linens and stored in the second bedroom. In its place was a small and confining hospital bed, about half the size of my mom's other bed.

The emotional abuse had begun.

I noticed that my mom had bruises on her arms, hands and bumps on her head from hitting herself on the rails of the hospital bed. Unfortunately, I never took pictures of these bruises, but I learned my lesson. She told me that she couldn't move in the bed and had trouble sleeping.

Within a week my mom was being drugged. I usually did not come to visit my mom early before work, but for some reason on this particular day on **May, 17, 2012**, I had this incredibly intense sense of anxiety pulling me to her house. It was almost like someone else was driving my car. When I walked into my mom's home, I saw her on the couch with her head slumped over on her chest. I thought she had fallen asleep, but found this odd, since after my mom gets up in the morning, she never nods off until mid-afternoon.

My mom was not asleep.

She was so drugged that she could not lift her head, she was drooling. I began to cry. The home health caregiver could not tell me what was happening. I didn't believe her.

Fortunately, I knew my mom was still under her primary care, the same doctor since 2000. When I called his office, his assistant answered the phone. It was a voice that I was very familiar with since I made most of my mom's medical appointments and I was also the one that had taken her to almost all of her medical visits. This time, the call was different. The assistant recognized my voice and in a very subdued and apologetic tone told me that the guardian had placed "a password" for my mom's medical information, and if I did not have that password, she could not speak to me about my mom. She apologized again.

This was the beginning of the illegal chemical restraint orders on my mom.

I let her know the condition in which I had found my mom, and asked her to relay the information to her doctor. I had to leave for work, but I made my mom coffee and gave her something to eat. The picture of my mom slumped over that morning is imbedded in my mind forever. She was helpless, but that's what guardianship is all about…rendering your victims helpless.

After my mom died, and when I got all her medical records, I saw the note for that phone call. It stated that her "daughter (Teresa) was very concerned about mom. We can't give info (Sic) to this daughter."

Diagnosing My Mom – Pick a Disease, Any Disease

From January 2000 until April 2011, my mom's primary care physician, Dr. Roger Velazquez never suspected dementia or ordered for her to be neurologically evaluated. There was never any note that she was "impaired" or needed a psychiatric evaluation. That is, until DCF was contacted on April 10, 2011. For 11 years, not one note of "dementia" was ever placed in her medical record, but after DCF was contacted, and on the day she was brought in for a routine physical, her primary care physician, Dr. Roger Velazquez wrote "dementia" on her medical records for the first time. Even though no follow up tests, proper diagnosis, MRIs or CTs were done to this point, the term was placed in her medical record.

In her October 10, 2011 psychiatric evaluation, my mom told the doctor (Dr. Adam Falchook) at Shands that she was "a little depressed" because her sister had just passed away. She was never diagnosed with schizophrenia, bipolar disorder, or any other type of depression; yet they kept saying that she was depressed, and continued to pump her with double and triple doses of anti-psychotic medications for schizophrenia, bipolar disorder and severe depression. I would be depressed if I was taken from my home, belongings, family, isolated and made to live in a lock down ward with people who truly had severe mental illnesses. During this same evaluation, an assistant to the emergency guardian, who had accompanied my mom to the visit, stated to the doctor that "the patient had been living alone and that some family members had been financially taking advantage of her." I had already been cleared for all three DCF charges brought against me. This was another false and slanderous statement against me, in order to justify the guardian's behavior.

Another alleged illness that my mom had was Parkinson's disease (PD). The average age of onset with PD is 62, and it occurs mostly in men. PD occurs over time, and mostly in people who are genetically disposed. Symptoms of PD includes tremors, slowed movement (bradykinesia), rigid muscles, impaired posture/balance, loss of automatic movements (i.e., blinking, smiling), speech changes, and writing changes.

In comparison, **Tardive Dyskinesia** (TD) is "a neurological disorder that causes involuntary, rapid movements of the face and body. The condition is a serious side effect of taking antipsychotic medications called neuroleptics, such as those taken to control schizophrenia"[11]. TD is a serious condition, but because there have not been many studies and research on this condition, it is estimated that at least 50 percent of people on antipsychotic medications will develop this disorder. Individuals experiencing symptoms of TD "have difficulty controlling their bodies and are prone to random, repetitive movements that can be mild or physically disabling." The condition can range from mild to severe, and it has no cure, and is usually common among individuals diagnosed with bipolar disorder or schizophrenia.

My mom was 94 when she was alleged to have "possible Parkinson's." She did not have the symptoms of PD, and at age 94, it would be a "red flag" for any qualified physician to diagnose her as such. She had the symptoms of TD. I am not sure where these neurologists and psychologists got their degrees. They gave my mom medications to control PD. Once again, she was misdiagnosed and pumped with drugs that she did not need. The last neurological report, January 9, 2015 stated "suspected Parkinson's." As with all her other "alleged" diagnoses, my mom was immediately placed on dopamine medications. Side effects of dopamine include negative effects on kidney function and irregular heartbeats. Kidney disease progression (renal failure) and heart problems were two of the health issues my mom developed under guardianship due to the overmedication.

They didn't know my mom, but they kept prescribing medications without observation for improvement or worsening of conditions, and then they wondered why she was developing jerky motions, and her legs would buckle underneath her. My mom was also in Stage III renal failure due to these drugs.

Even BEFORE the competency hearing, on May 24, 2011, my mom had numerous conflicting diagnosis by numerous medical providers. The guardians never kept her with one provider for any length of time. This is called "shopping around" when you want the

---

11

https://www.drugwatch.com/tardive-dyskinesia/

drugs and medications you are seeking for a purpose other than the health and well-being of the elder. It was a revolving door of doctors, nurse practitioners, and health care providers.

Below are just a few diagnoses. They including:

May 17, 2011 – possible dementia/Alzheimer's

October 10, 2011 – Shands Health; memory loss

March 20, 2012 – memory disorder

April 22, 2011 – memory problems

May 9, 2011 – Gentiva Home Health - "patient not appropriate for rehab. Patient has memory deficit."

February 3, 2013 – stable

April 10, 2013 – memory loss

May 8, 2013 – depression, memory loss

May 22, 2013 – memory loss, agitation

June 19, 2013 – memory loss, agitation

June 25, 2013 – decreased memory problems

August 7, 2013 – dementia

August 9, 2013 – order rollator (walker) – not done

December 10, 2013 – COPD (emphysematous change)

June 11, 2014 – COPD noted

August 4, 2014 – home health plan of care, (no Parkinson's noted)

August 13, 2014 – "<u>suspected</u> Parkinson's Disease, mild to severe dementia"

(Dr. Lance Kim), [medications started before MRI or head scan]; history provided "according to her daughter" (my sister)

September 16, 2014 – head injury with hip bruise

March 16, 2015 – dementia, Parkinson's

The Two Lock Downs – And They Said This Was a "Safe" Place? — How Many Falls?

All resident falls in a facility are supposed to be reported. However, they are not always noted in the residents' charts, especially if they are short staffed and/or forget to write things down. As mentioned above, according to a petition filed by the first guardian, my mom needed "necessary professional level of care in a safe environment."

According to her medical records, my mom fell **close to 30 times**, but not all of these resulted in hospital care or professional medical treatment even though some involved head injuries as not in the facility records. In addition, my mom was hospitalized in mid July 2013 with pneumonia. My mom was sick and with a fever for four days before she was taken to the ER. I had complained two days before her hospitalization. She was burning up with fever and coughing up green goop. The individual that called was not the guardian, or the nurse on staff, but one of the staff members.

Reports of falls included:

First facility:

June 20, 2012 – fall; taken to ER (26 days after being taken from her home)

June 22, 2012 – fall

September 11, 2012 – unwitnessed fall; family and friends notified,

November 5, 2012 – episode of choking,

November 11, 2012 – fall in bedroom; no concerns; guardian notified,

November 30, 2012 – resident fell in TV area, fell backwards on floor; taken to hospital

December 1, 2012 – resident found on floor near bed; continue to monitor

December 30, 2012 – fell and hit head on floor; taken to ER; UTI

January 24, 2013 – fell on right side, left hip contusion

February 5, 2013 – received call from DCF asking if resident has capacity to make her own decisions, advised patient is not capable

February 12, 2013 – found sitting on floor

March 26, 2013 – resident was found on floor of bathroom, "I was dizzy."

March 31, 2013 – fall, found on floor

April 8, 2013 – found on floor of bathroom

May 15, 2013 – resident called for help, lying on floor next to bed, **Belo notified, but "really didn't think it was necessary for her to go to the hospital…ice pack was applied**."

June 5, 2013 – chemical restraint form (Seroquel/Quetiapine – treats schizophrenia, bipolar disorder and depression); Robert Slaton, MD and Lisa Meyer, ARNP, Advantage Wellness, Gainesville, Florida.

July 14 – July 25, 2013 - pneumonia

July 27, 2013 – found on floor; family notified

August 1, 2013 – admit for pneumonia

August 6, 2013 – fall

August 13, 2013 – fall, sent to ER

Second Facility:

March 5, 2014 – fall; abrasion on left hand; "ice pack applied," [did not go to ER]

April 9, 2014 – laying on floor on her back near front door

July 6, 2014 – patient fall; PT ordered

June 11, 2014 – COPD noted, no CHF

July 8, 2014 – fall, UTI, admitted to West Marion (hospital); twitching movements, increased tiredness

Jul 10, 2014 – left hand wound

August 14, 2014 – refused MRI

September 11, 2014 – changed doctors

September 14, 2014 – to ER, resident on floor

September 16, 2014 – fell, bump on head, head injury with hip bruise, to West Marion

October 30, 2014 – eats 25-50% of meals; PT/OT extended

November 15, 2014 – loss of appetite and weight loss.

The Medications – Why Were They Drugging My Mom?

Right before DCF and guardianship, my mom's medications under her primary care **(dated June 15, 2010) were: Caduet, Metropolol, Vitamin C, and Centrum Silver**. Under guardianship, the medications kept changing with the "diagnosis." I found it extremely disturbing that each psychiatrist, neurologist, and other health care providers noted that my mom continued to have falls and balance problems, yet they KEPT PRESCRIBING drugs that made her continue to fall and have balance problems.

March 10, 2012 (still under primary care physician) - Hydrochlorothiazide (treats high blood pressure and fluid retention), Metropolol (for high blood pressure), Lipitor (treats high cholesterol), Lisinopril (treats high blood pressure), Citalopram/Celexa (anti-depressant).

April 9, 2012 – discontinue Klonopin.

October 26, 2012 - Hydrochlorothiazide, Metropolol, Lipitor, Citalopram/Celexa, Trazodone (anti-depressant and sedative), Tylenol, Klonopin (x2) (sedative), Lisinopril.

June 5, 2013 – chemical restraint order for Quetiapine/Seroquel.

July 25, 2013 – Tylenol, Atorvastatin (for high cholesterol), Cefpodoxime (anti-biotic), Cetirizine (antihistamine), Doxycycline (anti-biotic), Metropolol, Omeprazole (nausea and heartburn), Seroquel (x2) (anti-psychotic), Sertraline (anti-depressant).

August 5-6, 2013 (discharged from North Florida Hospital) – Cetirizine, Lipitor, Toprol (chest pain), Tylenol, Colace, Zofran,

Clonazepam, Seroquel (x2), Zoloft (anti-depressant),
Hydrochlorothiazide, Prilosec, Culturelle, Mineral Oil.

September 25, 2013 – Hydrochlorothiazide, Metropolol, Atorvastatin,
Tylenol, Clorazepam, Sertraline, eye relief, Docusate, preparation H,
Cetirizine, Omeprazole, Seroquel (x2), Doxycycline, Zofran, Artificial
tears, Cefpodoxime.

July 18, 2013 – Tylenol, Zofran (nausea), Seroquel (x2), Atorvastatin,
Zoloft, Prilosec (indigestion), Metropolol, Hydrochlorothiazide,
Mineral Oil (to poop), Colace (to poop),Cipro (treat infections),
Norvasc (treat high blood pressure and chest pain).

August 7, 2013 – new provider/doctor (Advanced Hospitalist Group,
Alachua, FL)

November 14, 2013 (a note in my mom's medical chart) – "…verbally
aggressive to other residents in mid-morning then begins exit seeking
and wanting to leave facility around noon time daily…banging and
trying to go out to 'go home'."

**[NOTE: From November 12 to December 24, 2013, I was
prohibited from seeing my mom, per a letter sent from the
second guardian to the second lock down facility].**

November 15, 2013 – increase in Clonazepam.

July 18, 2014 – Tylenol, Zofran, Seroquel (x2), Atorvastatin, Zoloft,
Prilosec, Metropolol, Hydrochlorothiazide, Mineral Oil, Colace, Cipro,
Norvasc.

October 12, 2014: Metropolol, Tylenol, Ammonium tears, Seroquel
(x2), Mucinex (chest congestion), Carbidopa (Parkinson's),
Atorvastatin, Sertraline, Ondansetron (nausea), Omeprazole (nausea
and heartburn), Namenda (dementia).

May 12, 2015 (under Hospice): Sertraline, Senna, Seroquel (x2),
Metropolol, Levodopa, Remeron (anti-depressant), Thorazine (anti-
psychotic), Lactulose (laxative), Scopolamine (for nausea and
vomiting), Methadone, Tylenol, Robinul (decreases
secretions in body).

Side Effects of Medications

Antipsychotics are also known as "neuroleptics," which mean nerve-seizing, "major tranquilizers, anti-schizophrenic drugs and chemical straightjackets"[12]. These drugs were originally developed to treat mental health illnesses in the 1950s such as psychosis and schizophrenia.

Antipsychotics are either typical (first generation) or atypical (developed since the 1990s). Drug companies market the atypical drugs as those with fewer side effects, but typically have the same side effects as the first generation antipsychotics.

All antipsychotic medications cause "akathisia," which is a "terrible feeling of anxiety, an inability to sit still, a feeling that **one wants to crawl out of his/her skin**".[13]

My mom use to complain that her skin itched all the time, and I oftentimes noticed that she would pick at scabs on various parts of her body. According to the Citizens Commission on Human Rights (CCHR), any antipsychotic in the blood stream can disrupt the body's normal biochemistry. These drugs tend to cover up or "mask" problems and wear out your body. According to Beth McDougall, M.D., CLEAR Center of Health, the patient can feel better for a short period of time, then these feelings decline. Dosing is usually increased, then increased again. Antipsychotics also damage nerve fibers, which results in "muscle rigidity, spasms, and various involuntary movements".[14]

A drug-induced side effect called *tardive dyskinesia* (TD) is a **permanent impairment** that includes "voluntary movement of lips,

---

[12] CCHR, 2010; http://www.cchr.org/sites/default/files/education/anti-psychotics-booklet.pdf

[13] CCHR, 2010, p. 6

[14] CCHR, 2010, p. 10.

tongue, jaw, fingers, toes and other body parts.[15] According to this study, patients 40 years and older are "three times as likely to develop the disorder as those under 40".[16] TD appears in about 5% of patients within the first year of being treated with anti-psychotics.

Another side effect of antipsychotics is called "neuroleptic malignant syndrome" and approximately 100,000 Americans die each year from these side effects, which include fevers, confusion, agitation, irregular pulse and blood pressure, and irregular heartbeat ."[17]

In psychiatry, drugs are used to treat and suppress symptoms, but the root cause goes untreated, and oftentimes worsens. For example, having been in a very dysfunctional 25-year marriage, and as a result of constant harassment under guardianship, I experienced some extreme health issues including insomnia, chronic stress and pain, and frequent anxiety/panic attacks.

Other side effects of antipsychotics include sedation, restlessness, stiffness/shakiness, heart problems, diabetes, seizures, dizziness, racing heartbeat, insomnia, agitation, anxiety, hostility, drowsiness, constipation, coma, inflammation of the heart .[18]

So when I say that my mom's death was intentional and pre-meditated, I am spot on. It was pre-meditated murder because they knew what the result would be for her. My mom did not have any of the mental disorders for which she was being treated, including Parkinson's disease.

Some of the drugs, and their side effects, that they were giving my mom included:

---

[15]

Dilip V. Jeste and Michael P. Caligiuri,Vol. 19, No. 2, 1993, p 304, Schizophrenia Bulletin, p. [16] 304

Jeste & Caligiuri , 1993, p 304 [17]

CCHR, 2010, p. 11 [18]

CCHR, 2010, p. 11

Seroquel/Quetiapine – is used to treat schizophrenia, bipolar disorder and severe depression. This medication comes with strict warnings about its use. [19]

> **"WARNING - INCREASED MORTALITY IN ELDERLY PATIENTS WITH DEMENTIA-RELATED PSYCHOSIS; and SUICIDAL THOUGHTS AND BEHAVIORS:** Increased Mortality in Elderly Patients with Dementia-Related Psychosis elderly patients with dementia-related psychosis treated with antipsychotic drugs are at an increased risk of death. SEROQUEL is not approved for the treatment of patients with dementia-related psychosis. Suicidal Thoughts and Behaviors - Antidepressants increased the risk of suicidal thoughts and behavior in children, adolescents, and young adults in short-term studies. These studies did not show an increase in the risk of suicidal thoughts and behavior with antidepressant use in patients over age 24; there was a reduction in risk with antidepressant use in patients aged 65 and older. In patients of all ages who are started on antidepressant therapy, monitor closely for worsening, and for emergence of suicidal thoughts and behaviors. Advise families and caregivers of the need for close observation and communication with the prescriber."

(1) **Antidepressants** (multiple doses given at one time), have some severe side effects. Common antidepressant side effects that are "particularly hazardous in the elderly include orthostatic hypotension, sedation, cardiac toxicity, and anticholinergic reactions."

Side effects of "selective serotonin reuptake inhibitors (SSRI) include agitation, anxiety, insomnia, sedation, gastrointestinal difficulties, and sexual dysfunction have been reported").[20]

---

[19]

http://www.rxlist.com/seroquel-side-effects-drug-center.htm

[20]

https://www.acnp.org/g4/GN401000141/CH.html

(3) **Clonazepam/Klonopin** is used to treat seizures, and may cause anxiety.[21]

Other side effects include:

* confusion, hallucinations, unusual thoughts or behavior; weak or shallow breathing;
* unusual risk-taking behavior, no fear of danger;
* unusual or involuntary eye movements;
* pounding heartbeats or fluttering in your chest;
* painful or difficult urination, urinating less than usual;
* pale skin, easy bruising or bleeding;
* new or worsening seizures;
* drowsiness, dizziness, problems with thinking or memory;
* tired feeling, muscle weakness, loss of balance or coordination;
* slurred speech, drooling or dry mouth, sore gums;
* runny or stuffy nose;
* loss of appetite, nausea, diarrhea, constipation;
* blurred vision;
* headache;
* sleep problems (insomnia);
* skin rash, or
* weight changes.

(4) **Trazodone/Oleptro** is often used to treat insomnia and depression together.[22] Some side effects include:

* Headache
* Muscle ache
* Nausea, vomiting, loss of appetite, or stomachache
* Constipation or diarrhea
* Dizziness or loss of balance

21

http://www.rxlist.com/klonopin-drug/patient-images-side-effects.htm

22

http://www.everydayhealth.com/drugs/trazodone

* Dry mouth or dry eyes
* Numbness, burning, or tingling sensations
* Confusion
* Blurred vision
* Ringing in the ears
* Nervousness or confusion
* Rash
* Sweating
*Weakness or fatigue

Serious side effects include:

* Worsening depression
* Suicidal thoughts
* A severe rash or hives
* Swelling of the face, lips, or tongue
* Chest pain
* Difficulty breathing
* Panic attack
* Irregular heartbeat
* Fainting
* Unusual bruising or bleeding
* Seizure

Trazodone also might cause some people to have <u>auditory hallucinations</u> while taking the drug. Basically, the person hears things.

<u>(5)</u> What is a chemical restraint order and when is it used?:

Chemical restraint is defined as "the use of any type of drug to restrict an individual's <u>movement or freedom</u>".[23] According to the above referenced website, it is <u>illegal for nursing homes</u> to "administer chemical restraint to residents unless they are used to treat <u>medical conditions</u> or prevent residents from <u>causing physical harm to</u>

---

[23]
http://nursinghomeabuseguide.com/abuse-injuries/elderly-restraints/chemical/)

themselves or other individuals. Federal and state laws aim to minimize the use of unnecessary drugs, especially chemical restraints." The site continues to state that there is no current drug that "has received U.S. Food and Drug Administration (FDA) approval for use as a chemical restraint." According to the FDA, approximately "15,000 nursing home resident deaths annually result from unnecessary anti-psychotic use." The chemical restraint order must be written by a physician, and it must also state the duration and reason for the order. Many states require a court order for these drugs to be dispensed against the will of the patient.

My mom was 94 years old. She could not run, and walked slowly. She never tried to kill herself or harm anyone around her. My mom was an angel. She was so peaceful and loving. All she did was pray and want to be with her family. My mom was given anti-psychotics from 2012 through her death in 2015.

For three years, the guardians and the doctors the guardians had in their pockets, drugged my mom. The drugs costs thousands of dollars per month, and are often billed to the federal government under Medicare, Medicaid or State Health Care Funds. The doctors get benefits of thousands of dollars for showing up and giving a 15 minute lecture in a fancy vacation spot. Some just get kickbacks until the feds find out and shut that down.

Withdrawals from antipsychotics are similar to other addictive drugs, and include nausea, vomiting, diarrhea, dizziness and shakiness, and cause death and permanent horrific conditions in the elderly.

102

Chapter 6

Life in the ALF Lock Downs

<u>The first Lock Down – Harbor Chase, Gainesville, Florida</u>

On **May 25, 2012,** my mom was drugged and removed from her home against her will. My mom's pastor was there the day they removed her from her house. She was transported to a lock down facility in Gainesville, Florida called Harbor Chase. It took almost another year to actually sell my mom's home, which was vacated for a long period of time. My mom could have stayed in her home during that time, and not have to be in a lock down facility where she was drugged, neglected and abused.

I was never told when or where she was being moved. My mom's health care surrogate (my daughter) was never notified of asked for her input. The guardian told my mom that they were going to paint her house  and she was going to a "hotel." My mom was never given the opportunity to integrate into the mainstream out of lock down. This is called "gas lighting" and Guardians and GALs often use it to further debilitate, depress and confuse the elderly, making any dementia worse–much worse. It is part of their plan.

On the day she was removed from her home, my mom STILL had not been medically diagnosed with dementia. She was re-evaluated in October 2011 at

Shands Hospital by a neurologist who stated that my mother had "age related memory loss," but never indicated dementia, Alzheimer's, that she needed a guardian, and/or needed to be a in a lock down facility. As was stated earlier, in her petition to remove my mom to a facility, the guardian stated that there were no other viable options for where my mother should live because of the supposedly large expenditures required to care for my mom in her own home. That is, my mom had nowhere else to live. The facility that was mentioned in this court order was not the facility where the guardian took my mom. The guardian presented a padded (inflated) budget of my mom's so-called expenses, if kept in her home, to the court. These expenses totaled to approximately $11,000 per month. The figure was totally incorrect and overinflated, for the sole purpose of having permission to remove my mom from her home. She claimed that my mom's electric bill was approximately $200 per month. In the 13 years my mom lived in her house, her electric bill never exceeded $100. I know because I use to pay some of them.

The cost for my mom to stay at the first facility was approximately $5,000 per month. In addition, the guardian also paid a "private sitter(s)" (one of her own employees or someone from a home health agency) to stay with my mom for almost one year after she was taken to the first lock down ward. The cost for both the lock down and private sitter was approximately $12,000 per month. Remember, the guardian had stated in her court order of February 13th, 2012 that it was **not** "economically feasible" to keep my mom in her home.[24]

---

[24]The real question in all of this, is how many thousands per month the Guardian and/or GAL and/or probate attorneys were receiving in kickbacks. These individuals are not required to report such kickbacks, generally.

It is very common in a guardianship situation to sell the home and place the disabled against their will into a nursing home where they will never see the light of day again. Nursing homes bill the government and the estate $5,000 to $15,000 per month, often provide kickbacks to the attorneys and guardians placing the

person there, but it only costs them $1,000 to house the senior, provide a staffing ratio of the worst sort of minimum wage employees of 1 to 10 patients, and feed these people the cheapest and worst food imaginable.

In order to better facilitate the fraud, one corporation owns the land, another the facility, another the equipment, another the nurses and staff, another the doctors, so that when one procedure or event is charged, it will result in multiple bills to insurance and the government, practically untraceable through a maze of corporations impossible to link together.

I learned very quickly that this is called "drain the estate."

My first few visits to the facility were uneventful. I mostly visited during dinner time. I understood why my mom was reluctant to eat the food. It was often cold, congealed, and unpalatable. In addition, my mom would not allow strangers to bathe her there, so I offered and was allowed to help my mom with bathing. This changed very quickly. The restrictive visitation orders began. I was not allowed to see my mom.

My Mom Starts Falling… All The Time

106

Less than one month after being admitted to the first Assisted Living Facility, my mom was admitted to the Emergency Room at North Florida Regional Medical Center for the first time on **June 20, 2012** with a urinary tract infection (UTI), dehydrated and malnourished. She was dirty, unkempt, and unbathed. I had been in a meeting at work and my mom had called me from the ER on my cell phone. I did not recognize my mom when I saw her, and even though

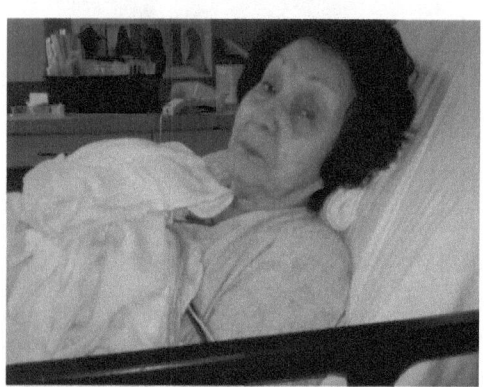

it broke my heart, I took a picture of her lying in the hospital bed.

Twenty-six (26) days, that's all it took from the day she set foot in the first ALF to the day she entered the ER for the first time.

I sent this picture of her neglected and abused condition to numerous private and public agencies, government officials, including to a former U.S. Supreme Court Justice. I soon learned that being outspoken only made the Guardian angry and more restrictive of my visitation with my mother.

There were only a few times in my life that I begged God to take me. Once, was when my daughter lay in a coma and on life support in February 2011. The other two times were when I was separated from my mom for six weeks in June 2012 at the hand of the first guardian, and then again in November 2013 at the hand of the second guardian.

If I could give one or two positive things that came out of these horrible experiences with my mom being under guardianship was that first, the relationship between me and my three daughters grew stronger, and second, their relationship with their grandmother also grew much stronger. Finally, one of my oldest and dearest friends, who loved and adored my mom and aunt, and whom I had known for more than 20 years, was able to get inside the facility. I mean she snuck in with her boyfriend, was able to see my mom and speak with her, then leave. She reported back to me immediately. Within a few weeks, she had signed up to <u>volunteer</u> and assisted at the first ALF on weekends, and only during times when I visited my mom. The guardian and my sisters never knew. She was my informant as to what was going on and what they were doing to her.

During the time my mom was at this first lock down, from May 25, 2012 - October 21, 2013, I was always kept 100% in the dark about what was happening with her health and her care. I was not allowed to contact my mom at the facility by phone.

In an email to staff on May 30, 2012, Casie M. Acosta, Director of Harbor Chase, instructed the staff: "Carmen is not 'allowed' to make phone calls out. (As per) Guardian Lynn."

In late June 2012 when I attempted to place a phone in my mom's room, at my expense, I was called and threatened with permanent visitation removal by the guardian on June 25, 2012. Somewhere, AT&T has a recording of the guardian screaming and threatening that I would lose permanent visitation if I did not disconnect the phone in my mom's room….a connection between my mom and the outside world.

This is isolation and emotional abuse.

The guardian stated that my mom had a phone in her room, but I was never given the number. Some of my mom's close friends were given bogus phone numbers in order to placate them. One of these "fake" numbers was the number of a pool house in Gainesville.

I did not know what doctor she was being taken to, what drugs they were giving her or how often they were giving them to her. After she passed, I was able to get all her medical records, including the one from this first facility. I discovered that even though my mom had been taken to the ER and hospitalized dozens of times, she had also been denied medical attention by the guardian on numerous occasions. My mom had fallen many times, with multiple head injuries that were ignored. The facility staff had called the guardian who refused to allow my mom to have proper medical care.

My oldest daughter, my mom's appointed health care surrogate, was never contacted, consulted, or allowed to make decisions for my mom. The guardian filed a petition in court appointing herself as my mom's <u>health care surrogate</u>. After my mom died, her will was deemed official and binding.

After reading so many guardianship abuse stories, I realized that the legal will, including designated power of attorney and health care surrogate, are ignored in probate court. We were not alone.

Between 2012 and 2014, I went through three different attorneys, none of which truly defended my legal rights to visit, and be with, my mom. My mom went through four guardians, including the first emergency guardian and three plenary guardians. The courts ignored the law, including FS 744, which dictates how a guardian in Florida should behave, treat the "ward"[25] and the family. I read so many articles about guardianship and found so many tragic stories. I found several Guardianship Abuse websites and organizations and read about the warning signs of an abusive probate guardian.

I was an educated woman, why didn't I know about this?

Why was this happening to vulnerable adults?

Why were they being taken away from their families?

But more importantly, <u>WHY</u> were they doing this <u>to my mom</u>? She had never hurt anyone. She was innocent. She was a true Christian woman. She was good, kind, and full of love.

In the four years under guardianship, I never heard my mom say a disparaging word about anyone – not my sisters, not the guardians, not the medical staff and doctors that had been drugging her. She prayed, and when I sometimes expressed anger at those who

---

[25]"Ward" is a fairly derogatory term that causes most family members to cringe when they hear that term. The term "disabled adult" is much more acceptable to family and friends.

were hurting her, she would say, "pray and leave it in God's hands, my daughter, leave it in God's hands."

I didn't understand where God was, but I did what my mom asked. I prayed with her.

Time after time, I went to the ER to visit my mom after her falls. Time after time, I was restricted from seeing her or my time was extremely limited when I saw her. I was not allowed to speak with medical staff about my mom's condition, or they were told to not give me any information.

I started bringing her Cuban food in the Summer of 2012 at the first lock down ALF. I brought her favorite soups, croquettes, café-cito, black beans and rice, pastelitos (Cuban pastries), and much more. We started doing arts and crafts, painting, and scrap booking. I brought old picture albums from her childhood in Cuba. She laughed and we laughed along with her. She could name everyone in the pictures, and I marveled at the detail in her stories – what was happening at the time of the picture, who was involved, and how she felt back then. My mom always recognized my children. She never asked "who are you" or "where am I," which is often typical in elders with dementia or Alzheimer's. She remembered their birthdays, and remembered where they went to school and what grade they were in. And this was WITH all the drugs they were pumping into her.

When several of my childhood friends came to visit in the second lock down ALF, she remembered them immediately, asked them about their families and children, even though she had not seen them in years. She always remembered my cell phone number, and that my daughters were in college. Eventually, the drugs they gave her took their toll.

That was what they wanted.

It was all pre-meditated.

My mom and I grew stronger in our love and connection. I brushed her hair and put on her make up during every visit, two things she enjoyed immensely. She beamed with pride and joy. I loved pampering her. We always prayed together, and I would bring her Communion on most Sundays.

As I mentioned earlier, Thanksgiving of 2011 was the last time I had my mom for a holiday at my house. Thanksgiving and Christmas of 2012 were difficult because we didn't have my mom celebrating with us. She was always the center of attention. My mom did not understand why she couldn't leave with me. She didn't understand a lot of things, but she accepted them. The holidays were never the same again. Each holiday, I would wake up thinking of my mom and how she would wake up alone, without family, on holidays like Christmas and Easter, which she had enjoyed with family.

How was this in her best interest?

I worked at the local Veteran's Administration for more than six years, and spoke with many Veterans about their Posttraumatic Stress Disorder (PTSD). I didn't understand what my mind and body were going through during the years my mom was under guardianship – why I constantly felt on edge, was always looking over my shoulder, could not enjoy life, was having constant nightmares, kept myself isolated because I didn't know who to trust (and with good reason), always felt anxious and uneasy, could not concentrate most days, and was always in an emotional state. I was constantly being attacked emotionally by the guardians and their attorneys, and most importantly, my children and I were being separated from one of the most important and loving people in our lives – my mom and their grandmother.

After my mom passed, I didn't experience nightmares for a long time until I had to deal with probate and her estate in late 2015 and early 2016. In essence, I was still dealing with the guardians, their attorneys and my attorneys once again. At one point, I went to see a grief counselor because the loss of my mom was overwhelming, as is in most cases with such a loss. I explained the circumstances surrounding the death of my mom, what I had experienced during her time under guardianship, and was feeling. She told me that the traumatic events I experienced prior to my mom's death were preventing me from grieving in a healthy way, and before I was able to grieve in a healthy way, I had to process and heal from the trauma of my mom's imprisonment under guardianship.

I am not alone. The same story happens to thousands of victims who lost their family member under guardianship.

These effects of what guardianship does to the family, who are also victims, include emotional and physical pain, sleep issues, and anxiety. You never fully recover from the stress and harassment. You never fully recover from the torture and abuse that you witnessed your loved one go through. But you do remember the really good parts, like the love, hugs and kisses despite the isolation and restrictions. The good always overcomes the bad.

Restrictions, Violations and More Isolation

When I felt that things could not get any worse, the guardian would always prove me wrong. I began to receive harassing letters stating that I owed thousands of dollars that I had "borrowed" from my mother. One was dated July 31, 2012 and the other one was dated December 17, 2012. These letters turned into an illegal law suit filed by the first guardian. It was eventually thrown out by a probate judge in January 2014. For example, in the July 31, 2012 letter, the guardian states:

"Within the month it will be necessary to discontinue the **private pay attendants** for your mother unless alternative funding is identified. My mandate is to locate all her assets to apply them for her benefit. I would like to identify all her assets to present a proper accounting to the court and also to assure the assets are properly managed for your mother's benefit. The urgency of this matter is high and I would appreciate a response from you by August 5th so that I might proceed further as necessary."

The guardian was not only paying the facility, but also admitting to hiring "private" paid attendants that she never asked the courts permission to hire attendants in the facility for my mom. The amount noted in this letter that I owed was $24,222.

The "Demand Letter" dated December 17, 2012 stated another amount, $10,612 + interest. Again, she demanded that I pay her, stating, "treble damages may be demanded plus attorney fees and costs if any person proves by clear and convincing evidence that an elderly person has been <u>harmed or exploited</u> by another."

Remember, I had already been **cleared by DCF** of all alleged exploitation charges. My attorney advised me to ignore both letters.

In the literally dozens of petitions and motions filed by the guardian, most of them were frivolous and included the proposed injunction against my two children in January 2012, her petition to put visitation restrictions on my dad's grave site on church grounds in 2013, restrict me from attending my dad's inurnment ceremony, and trying to find out if my mom's name was on the title of my truck so she could repossess it.

The first "Motion for Sanctions" was dated February 7, 2013, and was a law suit that named my mom as the person who was suing me and listed the guardian as "plenary guardian and attorney for the plenary guardian." My name was also listed as "Teresa H. Lyles," which is <u>not my name</u>. Remember, that according to the Examining Committee's findings on May 24, 2011, my mom did not have the right "to assist in the defense of suits of any nature..."

In this Motion, the guardian states that:
"Petitioner Lyles since the inception of the Guardianship of Carmen Tozzo has been unrelenting in efforts to interfere with the Plenary Guardian in the fulfillment of her court mandated and legislatively identified responsibilities...
petitioner's acts have resulted in emotional stress and financial costs for the ward which the ward can ill afford. The respondent respectfully requests the Court to enter an Order

awarding attorney's fees and costs directly against Teresa
Lyles."

The goal of this motion was actually to get more
money...for herself. I find it incredibly amusing that she
claims that I'm costing my mom "emotional stress and
financial costs for the ward" despite the fact that she admitted
in the first harassment letter that she is hiring my mom private
sitters in the lock down facility. There was no mention of the
drugging and isolation she ordered that was causing my mom
real stress. In addition, the guardian did not get official
authorization to sell my mom's home until 2013. My mom
could have at least been in her home for another year.
    In the end, the courts let her take the rest of the money.
Bad behavior is always rewarded in Probate and guardianship.
"Please Use English Only...."
    On **August 13, 2012**, I received an email via my attorney. The
email detailed several visitation restrictions, but my favorite ones are
listed below:
"1. ALL visits are to take place in either the TV area or one of the
dining rooms.
3. NO ONE AT ALL regardless of age is allowed to enter your
mother's room for any reason whatsoever. The staff has been
instructed to lock the room during your visiting hours.
5. Please use **English only** during your visits. Your mother is quite
competent in English and speaking another language around the
other residents is distressing to some and has exacerbated some of
their conditions, please be sensitive."

The guardian stated to me in an email,
        "indicate that you agree to be bound by them (visiting
        requirements) and that you understand that
        subsequent steps will be taken if and as necessary for

your mother's emotional and physical well being. **Until I receive such acknowledgement you may NOT resume visits**."

According to FS 400.011, "Nursing Homes and Related Health Care Facilities," my mom's rights in the NH included:

(1)(a)"the right to civil and religious liberties, including knowledge of available choices and the right to independent personal decisions;

(b) the right to private and uncensored communication, including, but not limited to, receiving and sending unopened correspondence, access to a telephone, visiting with any person of the resident's choice during visiting hours, and overnight visitation outside the facility with family and friends in accordance with facility policy...

(2)(h) the right to manage his or her own financial affairs...

(m) the right to close room doors and to have facility personnel knock before entering the room....

(o) the right to be free from mental and physical abuse, extended involuntary seclusion, and from physical and chemical restraints....

I could be wrong, but I thought freedom of speech was a U.S. Constitutional Right. This was a violation of the 14th Amendment, and my mom's rights as a resident of the NH. I lost almost two weeks of visitation for not agreeing to comply with this demand and the other demands stated in the email, none of which were ever approved by any judge or mandated by any court order. My attorney asked me to comply, but I refused.

However, my all-time favorite restriction was the email from **November 11, 2012**. My aunt, uncle, and father all had their ashes inurned on the grounds of Queen of Peace Catholic Church, Gainesville, Florida, at the columbarium behind the church. I frequently go to visit and pay my respects at this site, which is my right. Their ashes are on church grounds. However, on November 10, 2012, after visiting their grave sites, I entered the church where a Mass service was underway. I saw my mom with <u>two</u> caregivers. I went over to kiss and hug her then gave her $2 for the church basket, because the guardian **never** allowed my mom to have any money, including for church donations.[26]

The guardian sent an email to my attorney the following day (Monday, November 11, 2012):

> "Hope you are well. Sorry to bother you with this but I am informed that Dr Lyles arrived at Mass yesterday at Queen of Peace at which her mother was in attendance. This is quite a coincidence and regrettable as if it had indeed been unplanned <u>there was no need for Dr Lyles to approach her mother</u> whom she had schedule visitation only hours earlier, given her mother money and then left. Perhaps if it happens again Dr. Lyles could maintain her distance or simply **exit the Mass** without approaching her mother. For the record when we take Mrs. Tozzo to Mass we will never take her to St Pats which is Dr Lyles parish of registry precisely to avoid the possibility of such coincidences....Visiting with Mrs Tozzo for Dr Lyles is cancelled with immediate effect and will remain cancelled until Tues. November 20th.

---

[26]Once a guardianship has been ordered, all money must go to nursing homes, GALs, probate attorneys and court approved vendors. These people must be paid for one wicked hand always washes the other.

I am copying Harbor Chase on this note so they will
be informed. Thank you"

Again, <u>Freedom of Worship</u> is my Constitutional right. No
person has the right to restrict another individual from entering or
worshiping in any church. My mom was never allowed to worship in
HER own church again, the church where she had been a member of
and worshiped in, for more than 25 years. For the last two years of
her life, my mom was never allowed to enter a Catholic Church. She
lost another freedom, her First Amendment right to practice the
religion of her choice.

My mom was an extremely religious and spiritual person. I was
informed in an email, while my mom was still at the first lock down,
that the cost to transport my mom to church would be $75 for a
transport vehicle plus the cost of hiring an attendant. I was not
allowed to transport my mom in my own vehicle, which I had done
hundreds of times in more than three decades.

Again, no court order existed for the guardian to carry out
these restrictions.

To restrict my mom from attending church was like a sword
piercing her heart.

I asked my church to intervene, but they said that it was "out of
their hands." However, in early 2015, I saw that the first guardian had
placed an <u>advertisement in MY church bulletin, that she was an
attorney and guardian</u>, despite the fact that she did not have any valid
credentials for being a guardian. Trust me, I checked. After numerous
phone calls, and report for false advertising, I was point blank told by
every church official and the publishers of the church bulletin that
they could not "do anything" about the fraudulent advertising
because **she paid her fees to advertise**. To date, this person who
helped murder my mom, allowed abuse, and over medication, has her
"advertisement' in my church bulletin. Again, it's all about the money.

It's All About The Money, Money, Money….
Selling My Mom's House

After my mom was removed from her home, all her belongings were sold, discarded/thrown away, or distributed amongst my siblings. I was not allowed access to any of these items. My mom had bought an urn for her ashes about 10 years earlier, and this was also discarded. The only items that I was allowed to have from my mom's home were her old pictures from Cuba, and my old wedding dress that were left at the front desk of the first AL facility. My dad's ashes were also taken away by the guardian…or so she thought.

There is a funny story that came out of the madness and sadness of cleaning out, and selling, my mom's home, which I vehemently protested in court. After my mom moved to Gainesville, she bought a spot at Queen of Peace for their ashes in the Columbarium, but refused to inurn my dad's ashes at that time. In 2003, I had taken my mom to purchase an urn for my dad that fit in the space where both her and my dad's ashes would eventually be placed. My mom also picked out her urn at the same time.

Her wishes were **always** to be buried with my dad after she passed away. In the meantime, she wanted his remains in her home, on her dresser, close to her.

Fast forward to 2015 when I was making funeral arrangements for my mom.

I knew that my mom had bought an urn, but could not remember where or what had happened to it. I eventually realized that the urn had been discarded by the first guardian. I called several funeral homes, including the one that was closest to my mom's home. I was advised by the funeral home manager that my dad's ashes were still in their vault waiting to be placed in their proper burial place.

Then I remembered what happened back in 2003.

My mom had left my dad's ashes at the funeral home for safekeeping, but took both their EMPTY urns back to her house. The urn that was placed in my dad's spot at Queen of Peace did not contain his ashes. I had to have my dad's urn removed, sent to the funeral home to have his ashes placed inside, while simultaneously having my mom's ashes placed inside her urn. Despite all attempts to keep my mom away from my dad, and not allow her to attend the first inurnment ceremony in 2012, my mom got HER way even in death.

I laughed until I cried because it was exactly what she had wanted. I had forgotten the eternal bond they had with one another.

Forever in this world, and the next.

Only my daughters and several friends attended the inurnment ceremony at the church where my mom and dad's ashes were placed together. It warmed my heart to know that I had given my mom one of her last wishes. The guardians lost this battle. They would never win over their love for each other.

On July 31, 2012, the guardian filed a "Petition For Authorization To Deliver Cremated Remains of Ward's Spouse To Queen of Peace Catholic Community For Inurnment Service." Basically, the request was asking the probate court to determine if going to a religious ceremony for my dad (mom's HUSBAND of 43 years) was in **her best interest**, AND to restrict visitation to my dad's grave site on church grounds. The petition requested:

> "That the Plenary Guardian determine if the ward's presence at the service would be in the ward's best interest; That the family members be advised once the inurnment has occurred to **allow visitation** at the site and avoid possible confrontation between family members at the inurnment service."

In his response dated August 21, 2012, the judge's order stated,

"The Guardian has asked the Court to regulate notice of an inurnment ceremony and determine who, other than the ward, may attend. This request is beyond the scope of this Guardianship.

The Guardian may use the powers vested in her by the letters of plenary guardianship to deliver the cremated remains to the facility she believes to be beneficial for the Ward and determine the Ward's involvement and/or presence at a related ceremony."

My mom was never "allowed" to go to the religious ceremony because the court, once again, gave the guardian the right to violate her right to attend a religious ceremony. This was done "in her best interest." Only me, my daughters and a few close friends attended the ceremony in August 2012. No other family attended.

I objected in court to the sale of my mom's home, but my objections were ignored. The guardian and the probate judge did as they pleased. I was not even notified by my attorney of the second hearing regarding the sale of the house. Nothing is a coincidence or oversight in Probate Court. It is all deliberate and calculating.

After my mom's home was sold below market value, the money was placed in her bank account to continue paying for her abuse, neglect, and drugging at the lock down, a place where my mom did not want to be. My mother never saw one cent of the sale of her home. Meanwhile, she continued to be in an unsafe environment, at the mercy of the guardian, her attorney and my sisters. One of the duties of the guardian (FS 744) is to keep my mom in a safe environment and away from harm.

That never happened.

Not in 2012, 2013, 2014 or 2015.

Most of the residents at the first ALF had severe mental illnesses, such as schizophrenia, bipolar disorders, and aggressive/violent behaviors. The facility was co-ed, and many of the

120

residents wandered at night. They often wandered into my mom's room. She was always scared.

In 2013, my mom continued to experience falls, UTIs, and dehydration. I know that these are side effects of many of the medications they were giving her. I witnessed my mom with severe bruising all over her body (arms, legs, fingers, face). My mom's dentures and prescription glasses were taken from her. They tried to make it easier for her to fall and hurt herself. This is common practice in nursing homes because it makes the ward feel despondent, dependent and depressed.

On January 8, 2013, I came to the facility to visit my mom with one of my daughters. I immediately noticed how agitated my mom was acting. She kept saying that she had an argument with my dad. She refused to eat and I could not get her to relax or calm down. I asked one of the staff on duty (B. M.) if her medication had been changed or increased. They said "no" but they also noticed her unusual and atypical behavior. I became concerned, and a few minutes later another staff member told me that she had been attacked by a resident. This man, who I had witnessed on several occasions attack other residents, had gone after my mother. He had grabbed her and attempted to hit her over the head with a chair. This was told to me by one of the staff members and confirmed by my friend who volunteered at the facility. However, the same staff member wrote a note in my mom's record that she told me that "it never happened." My complaints to the guardian were ignored. The staff wrote a note (1/9/2013) in my mom's medical record,

> "Carmen's daughter…stated Carmen told her she had been in an altercation and why wasn't she told. I told her there was no altercation, it was a **misunderstanding** and Carmen was just walking by….she stated Carmen told her something about a chair. I wasn't aware of that so I told her it didn't happen."

If the staff member knew nothing about the incident, why didn't she just write, "I wasn't aware of the incident." But Instead, her words were, "I told her it didn't happen." I know what "it" means.

About two weeks later, this violent resident attacked several of the staff, and only then was he finally removed from the facility.

When I visited, I never knew when my children and I would be asked to leave or have our visits shortened. The guardian would often call as I was walking in the door and tell the staff to stop my visit. I would hear her on the phone.

Just days before my youngest daughter's high school graduation, in which the guardian would give me "permission" to take my mom to the graduation with extremely restrictive demands, another incident occurred at the ALF. On May 22, 2013, I arrived at the facility with my oldest daughter to see my mom. I was informed by the receptionist that the guardian was sending someone over to "serve me papers" during my visit. She had just hung up with the guardian when I walked through the door.

When I left the building, an old brown car was blocking my vehicle. I couldn't pull out of the parking space. The man who owned the car had been hired by the guardian to serve me papers. He was not in law enforcement or member of the courts, and he did not show me any credentials. He blocked me, and refused to move his car unless I signed the document, which indicated that I had received the paper work. I only agreed to sign that I had received them because I wanted to get home. It was the civil suit that was eventually thrown out in January 2014.

In this document, the first guardian was seeking to collect approximately $10,000 for money that I "allegedly" owed my mom. The law suit listed my mom as being the one who was suing me, and the guardian was acting on my mom's behalf as her attorney. The guardian was paying herself to be her own guardian attorney and a guardian. Remember, back in May 24, 2011, after the 65 minutes of being examined by three strangers, my mom lost her right to "to assist in the defense of suits of any nature against her."

After this incident, and the continued restrictive demands that this guardian was placing on me to have my mom attend my daughter's graduation, I declined to have my mom at my daughter's graduation. I did not want a repeat of my daughter's wedding the year before, and in light of the incident at the lock down facility with serving me papers, it sure seemed like it was moving in that direction.

Within a couple days, my attorney asked the first guardian for her resignation, and on May 28, 2013 in an email to the guardian, he wrote,

"after considerable reflection and research, I must request of you, on behalf of my client, that you resign as guardian in this case....involvement in a case of this nature over a lengthy and continuous period of time can cause one to lose perspective. This loss of perspective can, and often does, lead to a situation in which one allows emotions or other external factors not relevant to the case to interfere unduly in the discharge of those duties to which one is obligated. Please be advised that should you decline the request to resign as guardian, my client has authorized and instructed me to seek a court order removing you as guardian in this case."

On June 12, 2013, the first guardian resigned, filing a "Motion to Allow the Plenary Guardian to Resign." In this document, the guardian stated,

"the plenary guardian has been obligated to respond to interferences by one of the ward's children with frequency and intensity that result in fees and costs to the ward which ultimately the Plenary Guardian believes does not serve the best interests of the ward" and "the Plenary Guardian proposes the appointment of a Successor Professional Guardian."

My attorney and I were never notified of the selection, nor had access to, the next guardian.

In the court hearing on August 23, 2013, the presiding judge determined that the guardian acted improperly when filing the law suit and seeking monetary compensation as my mom's guardian and guardian attorney. Almost three years later, even though I had suspected all along, I found out that this first guardian had been involved and dictated all actions involving my mother until my mom's death on May 24, 2015. Despite this snafu and that she did not have any legal claim to my mom's money to pay herself as guardian attorney, the probate courts and judges did not really care about the law. Not only was she paid an estimated $60,000 + as a guardian, but she was also awarded an additional $12,000 to pay herself as a guardian attorney, although she never filed the paperwork in court to receive permission.

According to FS 744.108 (4) and 744.441 (11) (see below), there has to be "prior notice" of the fees being incurred. This never happened. In addition, as was stated by my attorney in an email to the first plenary guardian in May 2013, there is clearly a conflict of interest and also that she acted inappropriately (744.108 (3)) and (744.446).

The annual guardianship report was not filed from 2013 and 2015. The probate judge took no action against the guardian and their attorney (744.367).

744.108 Guardian and attorney fees and expenses.—

> **(3)** In awarding fees to attorney guardians, the court must clearly distinguish between fees and expenses for legal services and fees and expenses for guardian services and must have determined that no conflict of interest exists.
>
> (6) A petition for fees or expenses may not be approved without prior notice to the guardian and to the ward, unless the ward is a minor or is totally incapacitated.

744.446 Conflicts of interest; prohibited activities; court approval; breach of fiduciary duty.—

(1) It is essential to the proper conduct and management of a guardianship that the guardian be independent and impartial. The fiduciary relationship which exists between the guardian and the ward may not be used for the private gain of the guardian other than the remuneration for fees and expenses provided by law. The guardian may not incur any obligation on behalf of the guardianship which conflicts with the proper discharge of the guardian's duties.

(2) Unless prior approval is obtained by court order, or unless such relationship existed prior to appointment of the guardian and is disclosed to the court in the petition for appointment of guardian, a guardian may not:

(a) Have any interest, financial or otherwise, direct or indirect, in any business transaction or activity with the guardianship;

(b) Acquire an ownership, possessory, security, or other pecuniary interest adverse to the ward;

(c) Be designated as a beneficiary on any life insurance policy, pension, or benefit plan of the ward unless such designation was validly made by the ward prior to adjudication of incapacity of the ward; and

(d) Directly or indirectly purchase, rent, lease, or sell any property or services from or to any business entity of which the guardian or the guardian's spouse or any of the guardian's lineal descendants, or collateral kindred, is an officer, partner, director, shareholder, or proprietor, or has any financial interest.

(3) Any activity prohibited by this section is voidable during the term of the guardianship or by the personal representative of the ward's estate, and the guardian is subject to removal and to

imposition of personal liability through a proceeding for surcharge, in addition to any other remedies otherwise available.

(4) In the event of a breach by the guardian of the guardian's fiduciary duty, the court shall take those necessary actions to protect the ward and the ward's assets.

744.367 Duty to file annual guardianship report.—

(1) Unless the court requires filing on a calendar-year basis, each guardian of the person shall file with the court an annual guardianship plan at least 60 days, but no more than 90 days, before the last day of the anniversary month that the letters of guardianship were signed, and the plan must cover the coming fiscal year, ending on the last day in such anniversary month. If the court requires calendar-year filing, the guardianship plan for the forthcoming calendar year must be filed on or after September 1 but no later than December 1 of the current year.

(2) Unless the court requires or authorizes filing on a fiscal-year basis, each guardian of the property shall file with the court an annual accounting on or before April 1 of each year. The annual accounting must cover the preceding calendar year. If the court authorizes or directs filing on a fiscal-year basis, the annual accounting must be filed on or before the first day of the fourth month after the end of the fiscal year.

(3) The annual guardianship report of a guardian of the property must consist of an annual accounting, and the annual report of a guardian of the person must consist of an annual guardianship plan. The annual report shall be served on the ward, unless the ward is a minor or is totally incapacitated, and on the attorney for the ward, if any. The guardian shall provide a copy to any other person as the court may direct.

744.441 (11) Powers of guardian upon court approval.—After obtaining approval of the court pursuant to a petition for

authorization to act, a plenary guardian of the property, or a limited guardian of the property within the powers granted by the order appointing the guardian or an approved annual or amended guardianship report, may: Prosecute or defend claims or proceedings in any jurisdiction for the protection of the estate and of the guardian in the performance of his or her duties. Before authorizing a guardian to bring an action described in s. 736.0207, the court shall first find that the action appears to be in the ward's best interests during the ward's probable lifetime. There shall be a rebuttable presumption that an action challenging the ward's revocation of all or part of a trust is not in the ward's best interests if the revocation relates solely to a devise. This subsection does not preclude a challenge after the ward's death. If the court denies a request that a guardian be authorized to bring an action described in s. 736.0207, the court shall review the continued need for a guardian and the extent of the need for delegation of the ward's rights.

Again, the probate judges and courts did as they pleased with no regard to the law. However, almost 10 months after my mom's death, and after admitting in the judge's chambers that she did not follow proper court procedure, the probate judge gave her permission to take the balance of my mom's bank account – more than $12,000. More about this later.

The first guardian was resigning!!!

Finally, there is a God.

But…not so fast, here comes guardian #2, the goat farmer.

<u>Guardian #2 – The Goat Farmer</u>

On August 23, 2013, the official guardian baton was passed from #1 to #2. The hearing was scheduled for one hour in the court room, to discuss the next guardianship, the civil suit against me and my mom's future. However, my mom's future and her well-being were never discussed – only her money and how the guardians could get more of it was the issue at hand.

And of course, discrediting me, as usual.

A different judge presided over this hearing, who was as bad as, or worse than the others. My attorney and I protested the appointment of the second guardian, stating that we had not been notified, or had any part in, choosing her or even allowed to speak with her. It was noted in court that she did not have the proper credentials in place at the time of the hearing to become my mom's guardian, that is, the supportive documentation was not brought to the courtroom to attest to her competency as a guardian. She had been licensed to be a guardian in Marion County, but not Alachua County where my mom's probate case had been established.

At this hearing, the judge ignored my attorney's protest and appointed the second guardian anyway, only because the judge did not want the first guardian to continue making any more decisions about my mom. The judge allowed the law suit to continue into the second guardianship, even though my attorney showed that it was not valid. Again, the law and our requests were ignored.

Also at the time of the hearing, the second guardian, a goat farmer by trade, had more than a dozen wards under her care, and she had also been hand-picked by the first guardian. According to my recollection, I believe she stated in court that she had at least 18 wards under her care. When the judge appointed her, I saw my sisters "high five" the newly appointed guardian. My attorney saw the same thing. This was not a good sign. I had a bad feeling once again.

Even though it was never disclosed, and my attorney and I were not made aware of her medical condition, the second guardian had a terminal illness (cancer) at the time she was appointed as my mom's guardian.

According to FS 744, if a chosen guardian has an illness or is on medication that prevents him/her from effectively carrying out their duties, they are not allowed to step into the guardianship role. The second guardian <u>never had the authority to delegate any health care or</u> <u>medical decisions</u> for my mom. She had no court order or modified court order to isolate and prevent my children and I from seeing my mom. No court orders existed. The first plenary guardian was still running the show.

Once again, nothing is done by accident.

It is all planned ahead and pre-meditated.

From August 23 to October 20, 2013, I visited my mom during the same restrictive times – Tuesdays and Thursdays from 6 to 7 pm, Saturday from 3 to 4 pm, and Sunday from 10 to 11 am. I reached out to the 2nd guardian and asked if we could meet and discuss my mom's care.

She ignored me. Our meeting never happened.

More isolation and abuse were coming. Despite never knowing when I would be turned away or interrupted during my visits, my mom was always my #1 priority. She was always fed, her hair was always brushed, and I always put her make up on. She picked at the food in both facilities, but always devoured the healthy and freshly cooked food that I brought her.

I arrived on October 22nd for my scheduled visit, only to be informed by the Assistant Director that my mother had been taken from the facility the previous day (on October 21st). She was surprised because she stated that the guardian has told her that "all family had been notified."

For almost 48 hours, I did not know where my mom had been taken or if she was alive. The guardian refused to tell me where she was located or if she had been hospitalized or dead. While I was still at the first ALF on October 22nd, the assistant director called the new guardian on the phone. I told her that it was my right to know where my mom was located. Her only words to me were, in essence, that I had stolen money from my mom and she could not afford to keep my mom at the current facility any longer. My father use to say, "it's a broken record." Kind of like a messed up CD, but different. She never had a court order or court permission to move my mom.

So let me get this right…my mom was:

- removed from her home in May 2012, which was paid in full and she had <u>no mortgage payments</u>,
- placed in a lock down facility for about 17 months, where the expenses with "private sitters" totaled more than $10,000 a month, and then moved to ANOTHER lock down facility, because this was in her <u>best interest</u>?[27]

The deception was mind boggling, and it was also evil. My mom never stood a chance against the guardians, my sisters, and their attorney. I tried to fight according to the law, the legal way, but that got me nowhere. They fought dirty through a system that cared nothing about my mom, and who lost everything that my dad and her had saved and built throughout their lives.

In the blink of an eye, everything was gone. The most important thing which was completely wasted during this entire process was most assuredly her life.

The financial impact on my family was just as great. Between attorney's fees (three different attorneys while my mom was under guardianship), funeral expenses which are supposed to all be covered under guardianship, food, gas, caregiving for my mom while she was still in her home, clothes, make-up, essential toiletries, and gifts, I've estimated these costs total about $50,000. I never asked for anything

---

[27]It may be noted here that the cost to house a nursing home resident with a patient to staff ration of 10 to 1 and poor quality food is about $1,500 per month. The courts ensure that overpriced nursing home beds are filled to the max, the attorneys and court room vendors often take massive kickbacks to eliminate Protective Family Members, disparage them, false light them, and do everything in their power to keep the money and kickbacks flowing.

other than the expenses for the funeral – the urn and the casket for the Christian burial. I asked my attorneys multiple times to have this one item reimbursed. They never pursued it.

They ignored me.

However, my sisters were paid <u>out of my mom's own money</u> for Christmas gifts they bought "on my mom's behalf," for reimbursement of their attorney's fees, who put my mom under guardianship, and for the cost of my mom being in the first lock down, a place where she did not want to be. And I was the one being accused of taking her money?

This is irony in pure form.

I cannot say what other money was taken from my mom's estate and paid to the guardians and my sisters, because I was not allowed to see what was taken from my mom's bank accounts, what amount, and when. The supposed guardianship annual accounting documents are sealed unless you petition the courts to have them reviewed. By Spring 2016, I had become so disillusioned with the legal system that I refused to spend one more cent on any attorney for any reason whatsoever. My mom was gone and she was at peace, but her entire estate had been taken by the guardians, their attorneys and the probate courts.

I eventually found out that they had moved my mom to a facility about 45 miles south of Gainesville in Ocala, Florida. The new facility was in one of the worse neighborhoods in Ocala. Several days later, the new guardian filed a petition (October 24, 2013) to move my mother to the new one in Ocala, something they had already done <u>without the court's permission</u> or more egregiously, without notifying her family.

According to FS 744, the guardian does not need to give the court advanced notice if they move the "ward" to an adjacent county, and have 15 days to file a petition stating that the ward was moved. Again, no one asked my mom where she wanted to live. The move, as with all decisions made by the guardians, was NOT in my mom's best interest.

I arrived at the Ocala facility on Thursday, October 24th during my regularly scheduled time, 6 pm. My mom was sitting in the main room on the couch as I walked through the door. There was so much noise that I could barely hear myself talk. The staff seemed happy that I was there to be with her, and gladly welcomed me for the visit.

I went over to her, and hugged her for what seemed like hours, but I knew it was only minutes. She told me, "I don't understand why they are doing this to me." I held back tears and then I asked if we could pray the rosary. We prayed, and we held hands until I was asked by one of the staff to speak with the in-house physician. He told me that my mom was on two anti-depressants and narcotics.

He mentioned her Alzheimer's. I asked him if he knew who and when she had been diagnosed and he said "no, but she has it now." I found it odd that for almost four years while my mom was under guardianship, everyone, including the staff at both facilities, kept saying my mom had dementia, Alzheimer's, depression, Parkinson's and a number of other illnesses, for which she was never diagnosed, or properly diagnosed. On many occasions, such as with her Parkinson's diagnosis, the physician stated "possible" PD, but then started her immediately on meds to control PD. No MRI, no waiting to see if her condition was anything else, and no questioning why a 94 year-old woman was on so many antipsychotic medications.

Yet no one knew who had diagnosed her, knew when the diagnosis occurred, but they were giving her massive doses of medications that were contra-indicative of what her actual condition required her to take.

For the next 1 ½ years after her move to the second lock down, I made the 45-minute drive from Gainesville to Ocala on Tuesdays and Thursdays to see my mom. I never complained. She gave me peace and serenity whenever I visited her. No matter what I was going through at work or home, my mom blessed my life beyond belief.

With her, I was learning how to love myself again. She healed my internal wounds and scars. She made me laugh, and we always prayed.

The visits were short lived. Less than three weeks later, on November 8, 2013, I was approached by two facility staff members, while in my mom's room, who asked me to leave in front of my mom. Both individuals, one man and one woman, were aggressive and came in waiving a letter stating that this was "a court order" preventing me from being with my mom. I point blank told them that this letter was not a court order and it was not signed by a judge. More importantly, neither I nor my attorney had a copy of this letter. I did not read the entire letter, but only the part saying that "only Teresa Lyles" was not allowed to see her mom, and that my sisters were welcome at the facility. They threatened to call the police and have me physically removed if I did not leave– right in front of my poor mom who was crying and begging me not to leave her.

I was again stopped from visiting my mom. This time, there was no court order, only a letter from the second guardian addressed to the facility administrator stating that I was the only one not allowed to visit my mom. A letter (fax) dated November 8, 2013 said that I was restricted from seeing her. The letter was addressed to the facility manager, Bea Kelty, by Carol Preiss, and stated,

> "Teresa Lyles has not been authorized to visit by me or anyone else. She has been instructed that she not visit. Since it is my understanding she has visited the facility, it is my direction to you as Carmen Tozzo's guardian that Teresa Lyles **not be permitted** into the facility for any reason unless you have my authorization in writing." Finally, the guardian further states, "…Carmen Tozzo Julien and Elena Clark, both daughters of Carmen Tozzo, are permitted by me to visit their mother…no other visits for anyone have been authorized at this time."

I was not allowed to see or speak to my mom for about six weeks, until December 25, 2013.

The second guardian had <u>no court order for any of these restrictions</u>. The facility did not question the guardian. They did not have a court order for restricting me, but a note in my mom's medical file from the facility stated, "received instructions from guardian (via fax) for no visits from Teresa Lyles per court order. Staff informed."

In an email on December 19, 2013 to Ms. Virginia Griffis, my attorney stated:

> "I have not received a reply from you to my multiple inquiries regarding the continued restriction on my client's visitation with her mother. This situation is completely untenable, especially with the holidays approaching. We are now far beyond the period described in your letter of October 22. Continued restriction on my client's ability to visit her mother is completely unjustified. Please advise me no later than noon tomorrow as to what the holiday visitation schedule will be. In the absence of the provision of such a schedule, I will be compelled to seek <u>urgent redress from the Court</u> – redress which will likely include a request that the current guardian, like Ms. Belo, be removed from the case, either for incompetence or malfeasance (or both). Such litigation will require not only the attendance and testimony of all relevant family members, but the guardian and staff from the nursing facility as well. Additionally, it will result in the wholly unnecessary expenditure of legal fees to resolve an issue which should have been resolved a long time ago. **There is absolutely no reason to continue draining Mrs. Tozzo's limited funds unnecessarily.**"

In her reply, Ms. Griffis stated,
"Mrs. Preiss has communicated with the facility
regarding visits and to provide verification of her
authority to set visitation schedule and make visitation
decisions in the best interest of Mrs. Tozzo – this
became very necessary due to your client showing up
and demanding a visit unannounced and causing a
scene at the facility with the staff. This schedule is
necessary at this time for the overall mental and
emotional health of Mrs. Tozzo, to allow her to have a
regular calendar so that the staff and guardian can
schedule Mrs. Tozzo's other appointments....and her
other activities. The staff and the guardian are most
concerned with Mrs. Tozzo's overall stability,
happiness and health, which are greatly and negatively
affected by unplanned visits, disruptions by any of her
daughters who arrive unannounced at the facility and
cause a scene, and continuous lengthy phone calls that
interfere with Mrs. Tozzo's schedule."

However, there was no mention of all the falls, head injuries and
drugging with anti-psychotic medications that were "in my mom's
best interest" nor the fact that my mom was constantly being taken to
the ER, and the infestation of ants that was non-stop at the facility.
Not to mention, that during this same time, the co-owner of this
facility, and another facility in Ocala, were both under investigation
for operating without a license. More about that later.

The meals there were also sub-par, and included fried and salty
foods, such as hot dogs, fried fish, and "mystery" soups. In a
document dated September 30, 2015, the State of Florida Agency for
Healthcare Administration, addressing issues regarding the shutdown
of Memory Lane, noted that the average expenditures on meals was
about **$6.70 per day** – for three meals and snacks! That goes to show

you the quality of food they gave my mom, and how they did things "in her best interest." I use to spend between $6-10 per meal, usually dinner, every time I brought food to my mom.

Right before the New Year, I was able to get a hold of a personal letter from the guardian's attorney to my older sister detailing some trumped up charges that she would file against me, including her attorney's fees. I'm pretty sure that this is against the Florida Bar Code of Ethics. The accusations against me and one of my daughters were, once again, a smoke screen. Not only was my attorney never copied on this letter, but he was never contacted about any of my so called "disruptive behavior" at the lock down. For years, the guardians continued to accuse me and my children of "disruptive behavior" yet no police were ever called, and no notes were ever made by the facility staff in my mom's medical record stating as such. The disruptive behavior came from the other side, that is, the facility staff.

In a letter dated December 20, 2013, Ms. Griffis sent some personal correspondence to my sister. The letter she sent spoke to my sister personally about visitations to my mom. She stated:

"Dear Mrs. Julian:

I write to advise you of the visitation schedule for the Christmas Holiday and the month of January 2014, which modifies paragraph 5 of the order dated July 16, 2012.

Your visitations with Mrs. Tozzo during the last week of December and the month of January are to occur on Mondays during either the one-hour 1:00 pm to 2:00 pm block or 6:00 pm to 7:00 pm block. Please let Mrs. Preiss know which block you prefer as soon as you can.

Mrs. Tozzo is not currently allowed to be removed from the facility by anyone other than her guardian or staff, and all visits will occur at the facility. The Ward is not allowed to accept any phone calls.[28]

Any requests to change a day or time of visitation, which we expect to be rare, will require a minimum of 48 hours advanced notice by e-mail to the Guardian, Mrs. Carol Preiss.

We trust that you understand these rules are in place to protect Mrs. Tozzo, to confirm her visitation schedule as well as all other activities and appointments are coordinated in her best interests, to avoided disruptions to Mrs. Tozzo, the facility and other residents which cause emotional stress and unnecessarily strain the staff and resources of the facility, and to endure that each of her daughters have equal and regular access to Mrs. Tozzo as her condition allows.

As you can imagine, violations of the instructions and decisions of the Guardian and of the court order establishing the authority of the Guardian to set and adjust visitation (July 16, 2012)…increase the fees and costs incurred in this proceeding and unnecessarily deplete Mrs. Tozzo's funds. If my client has to deal with unscheduled visits or other violations or disruptions at the facility, we will **seek an order finding the violator in contempt and seek an award of attorney fees or other costs incurred against them**.

On October 29, 2013, Teresa Lyles and her daughter, Barbara, arrived unannounced at the new facility

---

[28]Federal Guidelines for Nursing Homes require patients be provided with a phone in their room at all times and be freely allowed to make or receive calls.

despite the letter of October 22nd that I sent with my client's instructions regarding the prohibition of visitation with Mrs. Tozzo for a temporary period **for her own adjustment**, medical needs and welfare. They created a commotion at the facility which disrupted and greatly affected Mrs. Tozzo, and she remained greatly agitated after they left. It was later discovered by the facility director that Teresa Lyles had previously gained access to the facility by posing as a Shand's nurse and misleading staff. On November 7, 2013, Mrs. Lyles again showed up at the facility, despite the Guardian's instructions prohibiting visitation temporarily, with a local law enforcement officer demanding access to the Ward. Mrs. Tozzo saw this occur and became very upset. Also, the facility has advised the Guardian that family members on various occasions have attempted to **contact Mrs. Tozzo by telephone during the time that they were prohibited from visitation or contact with her**.

Additionally, Teresa and Barbara Lyles have subjected the staff of the facility to verbal abuse, harassment, needless confrontations and interference with their work, as well as disruptions to other residents. This will serve as notice that any future violation will result in a motion for contempt being filed against the violator without further notice.

Thank you for your cooperation. We wish you Happy Holidays and a Happy New Year !"

I found it very odd that an attorney for all three guardians would not only send my sister a personal letter stating my alleged "violations," of which there was no evidence, but also letting my sister know that she would <u>attempt to seek legal action</u> against me with trumped up charges. This is a very blatant conflict of interest and an attempt to seek retribution for personal and financial gain. I believe she also billed for this letter.

The court order dated July 16, 2012 was ONLY for the first guardian, Marilyn Belo. This order was **never** amended to include the second guardian, Mrs. Preiss. The letter of October 22, 2013 was never part of a court order or motion filed in court for restrictive visitation measures. The so-called "for her own adjustment, medical needs and welfare" about my mom, probably refers to the continued drugging and neglect on my mom that they did not want me to see. My mom was agitated because <u>she did not want me and my daughter to leave her</u>. She wanted to go home with us, and she lived in fear.

Ms. Griffis' statement about me posing as a nurse is incorrect. My oldest daughter is <u>actually a nurse</u>, but I do have a Ph.D., and I'm sure the facility director was confused by our professional degrees and experience. It must have been mind

boggling for them to keep all of this straight. The harassment was from the facility staff against me and my visitors, not the other way around, as my guest visitors (witnesses) would vouch.

I don't remember much about those next six weeks without seeing my mom, only that there were several emails back and forth from my attorney to the guardian's attorney about reinstating my visits. I kept telling my attorney that there was NO COURT ORDER restricting my visits. He did not put up much of a fight for me. He allowed my visits to be suspended. I cried and I raged every night. I had dreams about my mom. I kept having these bad feelings.

On the evening of December 25, 2013, along with my three daughters and son-in-law, we walked into the facility for the first time since November 13, 2013. Even though what I saw was a shell of my mom, I could not stop kissing her and holding her hand. She had lost a lot of weight, probably close to 25 pounds. She looked extremely pale, gaunt and tired.

She looked drugged.

We opened Christmas presents and she was excited about all of them, and having her daughter, three granddaughters and family around her.

As 2014 approached, I wondered how often the visitations would continue. I saw from the mandatory sign-in sheets that my sisters were coming more frequently – three or four times a week – but I was never notified of the change from the guardian. They had been allowed to visit, per an email from the second guardian to the facility, my mom during November and December 2013, while I was still on restriction. This is bias and a violation of FS 744.

There was never "impartiality" with the three guardians. They always contacted, and consulted with, my sisters on any and all issues regarding my mom via text messages, emails and personal letters. I never received the same courtesy. Actually, it was the opposite – they kept me in the dark, and fought me with my mom's money to keep me and my children away from her. Their goal was to emotionally and financially bankrupt me.

In early January 2014, the second guardian's health turned for the worse, and on January 24, 2014 she passed away. An emergency guardian was put in place, but she did not have the proper license to be my mom's guardian either.

My mom was <u>without a guardian</u> from January 24th, through almost the end of April 2014. Nobody was taking care of my mom, and seeing to her needs and basic care. No one was making any medical decisions for her, but she <u>continued getting the drugs</u> that made her sicker, and continued to debilitate her. Again, no one contacted my daughter for medical decisions as her grandmother's legally appointed health care surrogate. An emergency hearing could have been requested by the judge.

<u>Guardian #3 Enters the Picture</u>

The best compliment that I can give to the third, and last, guardian (Andrea "Andy" Wolfkill) is that she gave me "permission" to sit outside on the porch with my mom at the second ALF and let her get fresh air and let the breeze hit her hair and face. We had the freedom to speak about anything and everything – in Spanish and English. She loved eating on the porch. She didn't even mind the noise from the neighborhood.

My mom and I talked about everything – love, life, children, grandchildren. One of the best things my mom and I started doing as part of our visits during this time was peruse through fashion magazines. I subscribed to, and shopped at, Chico's catalogs and she loved the clothes!! She would look at each clothing item and try to "mix and match" outfits according to her taste. We talked about where we could wear them (church, dinner, the beach) and if she would be able to afford it. During this time while she was at the second ALF, I gave her several items of clothing from my closet. If I wore it to our visit and she liked it, I would gladly give it to her. Unfortunately, whatever it was that I gave her would be gone by my next visit. My mom also learned how to operate my smart phone and "swipe" to access an app. We listened to music on YouTube, and sang along to songs such as "Guantanamera," and "Cuando Sali de Cuba."

It's Not **What** You Know, It's **Who** You Know

The chief financial officer (CFO) of Memory Lane in Ocala, Florida (Southeast Senior Care Management Group, LLC) is listed as John Cheney, and the corporate director is listed as Anita Hellmig. Cheney was identified as the owner and manager, and Hellmig as co-owner of the Heritage Senior Living facility. Heritage and Memory Lane are "sister" facilities.

As a result of a March 11, 2014 survey by the Florida Agency for Healthcare Administration, Cheney and Hellmig were cited as "knowingly operating an unlicensed assisted living facility" (Heritage Senior Living facility), located in Ocala, according to FAHA Case #2014004024.

Documentation also showed that a civil Complaint for Eviction was served on or about September 9, 2014 for Memory Lane, Ocala, Florida, which is where my mom resided at the time. FAHA documents state that Memory Lane "improperly combined resident care FTEs and salaries with dietary FTEs and salaries. The facility further improperly included these FTEs and salaries…." The average monthly per person meal budget for females 71+ is $203.20, or about $6.76 per day.

From June 11-14, 2013, the FAHA began their investigation of the unlicensed Heritage facility. The Agency interviewed Hellmig on June 11, 2013 and issued her a "Notice of Unlicensed Activity" letter, which she signed.

On June 14, 2013, the agency interviewed Andy (Andrea) Wolfkill, who was the Power of Attorney (POA/guardian) for four residents at the Heritage facility. Ms. Wolfkill stated in the interview that "John Cheney is part owner of the facility and **she has been friends with him for years**. She **knew** the facility was unlicensed."

Memory Lane was also cited as sending at least one resident to Heritage. As of August 3, 2015, the facility had no staff and no residents. The facility was abandoned.

Cheney was based out of Georgia and was arrested on **April 8, 2015 for 12 first degree felony counts for forgery**. He failed to pass a background check. Wolfkill is also from Georgia.

It's not what you know, it's who you know.

Some of the violations cited included: storing medication in unlocked containers, providing health care appointments, food, and housing for residents. Marion Country Fire Rescue fire inspector's letter dated February 24, 2014 listed 12 violations, mostly related to resident safety.

My mom was handed over to a guardian who had a long time **friendship with** a man with **12 first degree felony convictions - a criminal**.

My mom was handed over to a guardian who was knowingly involved with people who had sketchy business dealings.

My mom was handed over to a guardian who knew what would happen to her at the facility. When my mom was placed in Memory

Lane on October 21, 2013, there was an ongoing investigation at the sister facility.

They kept taking my mom's money even though the facility wasn't licensed.

They kept taking my mom's money even after Cheney was arrested.

They had to do something…my mom's death was the only option.

More smoke screens.

There was an ongoing investigation at the time she became my mom's third guardian. A simple Google search of Andrea Wolfkill by the probate courts would have revealed her involvement.

The probate courts failed my mom yet again.

My mom was never allowed to have a calendar in her room. I bought three of them for her, but they were all removed from within a few days after she got them. The staff would always say "another resident" took it, but I knew that wasn't true. I would also buy my mom make up, and basic toiletries, which also went missing within a week after I gave them to her. Again, the staff stated that "another resident" probably took the items. To prove my point, I bought my mom some items such as hand sanitizer, tissues, toothpaste, lip stick, and other similar items. I placed these items inside a make-up bag and purposely hid them under several layers of my mom's clothing, on the bottom shelf of her dresser. Within a week, the items were gone.

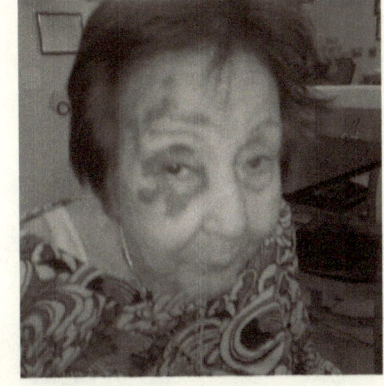

I was the only one who knew where they were. No one saw me place them in that secluded spot.

However, at the second facility, the bruising, UTIs, and constant drugging continued. As a result of several years of antipsychotic medications, Seroquel and other hard drugs, my mom developed an irreversible neurological condition.

I did a lot of research and refused to believe she had Parkinson's disease. I found a disorder called **tardive dyskinesia (TD)**, which I had never heard of before. TD is an <u>irreversible neurological disorder</u> that occurs in people who have been given anti-psychotics for years as I have described earlier. Interestingly, they kept telling me it was Parkinson's, although she was never properly diagnosed with Parkinson's, and did not develop the tremors or multiple symptoms associated with someone with PD.

On March 7, 2014, my daughter and I entered the facility. I stopped to speak with one of the staff, and heard my daughter gasp, "oh my God, what happened?" I turned to see my mom with bruising around her eye and forehead. She had a huge bruise and bump on her right knee and another bump on the top of her head. At first, I was told that it was "rug burn." I sent the picture to the guardian (not yet officially appointed) and asked for an investigation of the incident. She told me that my mother was "fine" and had instructed the staff to

"put ice on it." I also sent the picture to my attorney. My mom was not examined by a doctor for more than 24 hours. There was no report or investigation of the incident. She was never taken to the ER or seen by a neurologist within the first 24 hours. This was not the first time at this facility that I found my mom with bruising. She also developed sores on the top of her head and arm. I realized after her death that these sores were side effects of the medications she was taking.

As with the other guardians, my mom was not given medical attention on many occasions. As with the other guardians, my daughter was never consulted on any decisions regarding her health care decisions. Remember, my mom did not have an official health care surrogate, power of attorney or legal guardian for

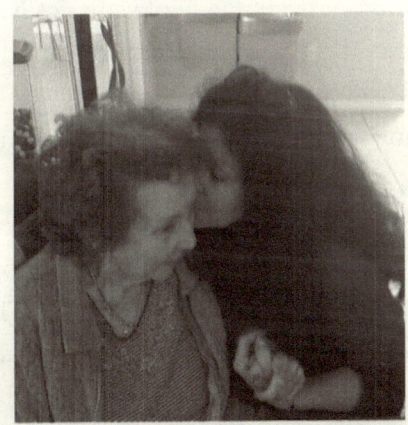

more than three months. This third guardian was given permission to make medical decisions, but she was never officially appointed as a health care surrogate. And as with the first guardian, my daughter was never contacted for a hearing or made aware of this decision.

Although I did not meet this last guardian for many months, nor was I ever contacted by her via phone or email, I discovered after my mom's death and after the final guardian accounting was submitted, that this last guardian and her attorney were in constant contact with the first guardian for consultation. The attorney for this last guardian was also the attorney for the first and second guardians. I think this would probably be considered a conflict of interest.

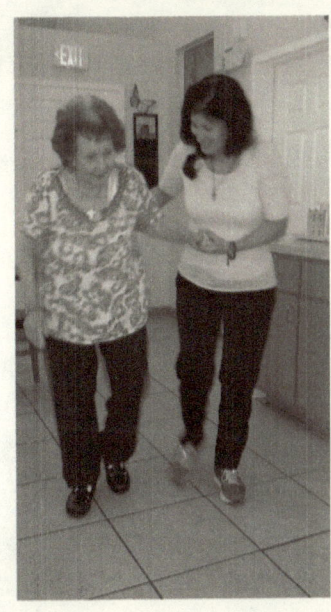

In late August 2014, I was emailed by the guardian stating that she had to discuss an important issue regarding my mom's health. I found this odd because I felt that my mom had been doing great. She could walk, she was gaining weight, and she felt good and looked good despite the continued and forced drugging. I think that was the problem, my mom was getting better physically. They didn't like that. Plus, as mentioned earlier, Memory Lane and Heritage were now both under scrutiny by the Florida Agency on Healthcare for multiple violations, including operating without a license.

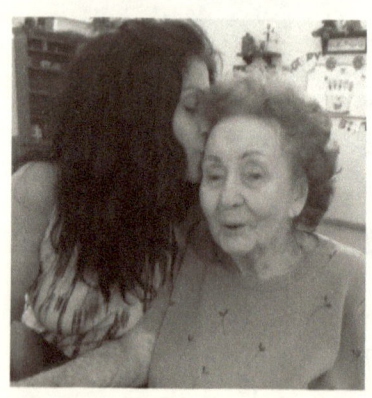

Eventually, my mom's walker was taken away, and she was forced to use a wheel chair most of the time. There was no padding on the wheelchair, which increases the chances of pressure ulcers, despite asking many times for this to be corrected for her. One hour was just not enough to be with her. It was never enough, especially when I used to spend entire days lying in bed with her, sleeping next to her, holding her hand. I can still remember how her hair smelled and the texture of her face, and how her hand felt in mine.

The last guardian let me know that she wanted to put my mom under hospice care. However, I vehemently objected stating that my daughter, her health care surrogate, and I disagreed and felt that she

did not qualify for hospice. I sent her a copy of the will and designated health care surrogate. She never called me again.

Interestingly enough, right about this same time was when the facility's license to operate was revoked. From about September 2014 until my mom's death, the facility was operating without a license. I discovered this when I went to collect my mom's belongings about two months after she died. The building was abandoned, and then I saw a news report exposing the details. Although I never recovered any of my mom's belongings, and no final inventory was ever submitted to the courts, I did get her medical records.

I got all of her medical records.

Our last Thanksgiving and our last Christmas together in 2014 was precious. I look at those pictures all the time. My children, my son in law and I, opened presents with her. She was smiling, she was happy and she was full of love.

I remember a visit between Thanksgiving and Christmas of 2014, when my youngest daughter and I went to see her. The facility van was gone and many of the residents were not there, but my mom was waiting for us by the door, sitting in her wheelchair. The staff told me that many of the residents had left over an hour before I arrived and were "driving around to see the Christmas lights." But my mom refused to go because she told them, "my daughter is coming."

She always knew.

She always waited for me, until that last week of her life.

On February 20, 2015, three months <u>before</u> my mom passed, the owners of the facility (Southeastern Senior Care Management Group, LLC) filed for bankruptcy in Georgia Northern Bankruptcy Court, where the owner was based. I find it hard to believe that no one, including the guardians, their attorney or the facility manager knew what was happening. And if they didn't know, it was their JOB to know and keep my mom safe.

On March 5, 2015, my mom was admitted to West Marion Hospital for the last time. She was admitted for a UTI, dehydration and back pain. I stayed with her for as long as I could the first night, but they did not admit her until after midnight. I went after work the next day, Friday, and stayed with her for quite a while. During that visit, I had several discussions with her nurse, doctor, and a wonderful physical therapist named Ivan. I asked him if he could recommend PT for my mom who they claimed could not use a walker and needed a wheelchair full time. The PT assisted my mother out of bed and she walked up and down the hallway, by herself, several times. I was not allowed to help her, she did it all by herself. The PT asked her numerous questions about her life, her family, and herself while they were walking. He indicated that he couldn't recommend PT because she was perfectly capable of getting up and walking. In her medical records, it states that she had "possible mild dementia."

The next day, Saturday, I found the guardian in the room, talking on the phone with one of my sisters. My mom looked very uncomfortable, but when she saw me, her face lit up. We held each other tight. The first thing the guardian said to me was, "I'm getting her doctor to put your mom in hospice. She's 95 after all." Not only was I angered at her statement, but completely flabbergasted that she had the audacity to say such a thing in front of my mom. She was heartless. Moreover, my family is staunch Roman Catholic and this is never permitted. The decision to pass over is strictly between God and the soul involved. The woman was a guardian and knew nothing of this basic concept.

The following day, Sunday, I visited my mom again before she was released back to the nursing home. She didn't want to go back there. As with the end of any hospital visit, she always begged to come home with me. As I left the room and was waiting for the elevator, I was approached by someone from my mom's care team. I thought she was a social worker, but I wasn't sure about her role. She described the incident of the guardian attempting to convince my mom's attending physician to sign my mom over to hospice, but he refused. They all agreed that although my mom had some medical issues and was well into her 90s, she was still fairly healthy and nowhere near ready for hospice. I hugged her and thanked her.

Hospice – The End, My Friend

My mom was released on March 8, 2015 from West Marion Hospital, after I was told that she would not be admitted to hospice by her attending physician and staff.

On March 11, 2015, the third guardian ordered a hospice consult, and they admitted my mom into Hospice on March 12, 2015 by Dr. Eladio Dieguez. In the hospice assessment of patient dated March 12, 2015, it was stated that "patient has no family" and also "patient has no significant others."

John Chaney, Ms. Wolfkill longtime "friend" was about to be arrested for 12 first degree felony convictions.

I guess the guardian finally found a physician who would agree to murder my mom. I've stated many times throughout this story, I always had feelings or premonitions with things regarding my mom.

Somehow, I always knew that things were going to happen before they happened or as they were happening. My mom and I were that close and in tuned with each other's feelings and emotions.

About two weeks or so after she was released from the hospital, my mom started saying some weird things to me, like "I don't understand why these women keep visiting me." I would ask her "who" but she couldn't answer and would say that she didn't know. I had a friend who had worked for hospice in Gainesville for many years. I told him of my suspicions. I told him I was worried. He encouraged me to contact hospice in Ocala because they could not refuse to speak to me, I was my mom's daughter after all.

He was so wrong.

I contacted Hospice of Marion County, and confirmed my greatest fear, that my mother was under their care. They could not talk to me about my mom because I wasn't "on the list" of family who they could speak with. Both my sisters were on the list. I faxed them a copy of my mom's will and designated health care surrogate. I explained what the doctor had said at West Marion, but none of that mattered to them.

They ignored me and my concerns.

The web site for Hospice of Marion County[29] states that "at Hospice of Marion County, our <u>mission</u> is to provide exceptional support for patients and their families," and that "our goal is to provide this professional service of <u>pain relief</u> and symptom management."

While under hospice, my mom's medical record stated the following about her pain:

      April 6, 2015 – pain, complaint

      April 7, 2015 – pain; headache & shoulder

                    pain

      May 18, 2015 – complaining of pain

      May 19, 2015 – has pain

      May 20, 2015 – soft tissue swelling; knee pain;

      May 21, 2015 - pain

Her medications under Hospice included (May 12, 2015): <u>Sertraline, Senna, Seroquel (X2), Levodopa, Remeron (anti-depressant), Thorazine, Lactulose, Scopolamine, Methadone, Robinul (reduces secretions before surgery)</u>. They kept switching, changing, increasing, and decreasing her medications. The last month of her life she was in constant pain, according to staff notes in her medical record.

Again, I found it very interesting and odd that back in May 17, 2011, Ms. Brasington, the attorney for my sisters and the first emergency guardian, stated that my daughter <u>could not be my mom's</u>

---

health care surrogate, but both my sisters were always allowed to bring my mom to medical appointments, and also allowed to consult, discuss, and diagnose with health care providers about my mom's medical treatment for four years without court approval or authorization. The authorization came only from the guardian, to make sure that my mom was kept drugged, confused, and immobile. This also includes a note in Hospice records on April 8, 2015 that stated, "continue with emotionally supportive visits to patient, and **contacts** with patient's daughter, Elena."

A staff member at the lock down facility confirmed that my mother was being seen by a hospice nurse, but I never met any of the hospice staff. Evidently, their visits would "coincidentally" never coincide when I came to see my mom.

They never contacted or spoke to me.

They never reached out to me.

This was done on purpose and at the request of the guardian who had no court order restricting me.

My attorney filed an emergency petition for me to have access to hospice. But this took time and time was not on my side. Less than two weeks after my attorney filed an "Urgent Motion for Interim Judicial Review of Guardianship" so that I could get "permission" to speak with hospice, they murdered my mom.

I say murdered because that is exactly what they did, slowly, starting in 2012.

They drugged her with medication that was intended to kill her, and they knew it.

They drugged her with medication that would subdue and affect her cognition.

They drugged her with medication for illnesses and conditions she did not have.

I remember her last birthday, her 96th, on March 24th. I have a picture of her blowing out candles. She loved the cake I brought her. She loved the presents. I remember our last Easter and Mother's Day as if it happened yesterday. It doesn't seem like more than a year ago.

On Easter Sunday, April 5th, she begged me to take her to church, a place that brought her comfort and solace, but I told her that I couldn't. She asked why, and for probably the hundredth time, I told her why. She was really quiet and looked sad, but she turned to me

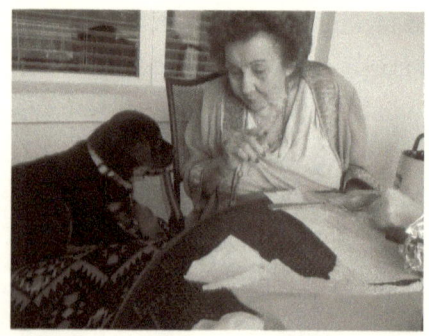

and said, "you have to forgive them, you have to forgive your sisters, and you have to speak to them again." The tears began to flow as I held her hand. I could never lie to her, so I told her that I wasn't ready now, but promised that one day I would. She seemed satisfied with this answer.

On Mother's Day, we brought our Rottweiler puppy, Bill, to see her for the first time. My mom was so excited. He was so little then, but such a precious and fluffy surprise for her. She wanted me to keep bringing him back.

On Tuesday, May 19th, I entered the facility looking for my mom. She wasn't waiting for me as she always did. I found her in bed looking like a zombie. She could not get out of bed, she was barely responding to me, she could barely speak, and seemed incoherent. I started crying. I became extremely anxious. My friend and her boyfriend, my guest visitors that day, arrived a few minutes after me. They witnessed her condition and state. The facility manager threatened to <u>call the police</u> because I asked her what Hospice was doing to my mom.

I left my mom early that day, and my heart was broken. She

needed rest, and she wasn't well. However, I returned the next day and she seemed more alert, and fairly coherent. She complained of pain in her leg. I took off her shoe and saw a huge blister and a severely swollen foot and ankle. The shoe had been forcibly put on
my mom's foot. It caused her extreme pain. It almost seemed like her foot was shoved into her shoe without care for her comfort. I reported this to the manager and said she did not know "how that got there."

No one seemed to know anything about anything.

On Thursday, May 21st, my mom and I sat outside. She was happy and in a great mood. She ate all her food and seemed like she was her old self. We took our last pictures that day, our last selfies. I did all the things that I always did. I put cold cream on her hands and face. I brushed her hair and put on her make-up. We held hands, kissed each other and
looked at a photo album. That was the last time my mom and I had a conversation. It was the last time we sat and laughed and ate together. In her medical record for May 20, 2015, there is a note that states my mom "appears more confused, unable to identify her daughters by name." Not only did she recognize and socialize with me the following day, but my youngest daughter also came to see her about an hour after I left. She recognized my youngest daughter, who also came to her about an hour after I left. She recognized my daughter,

as she always had, and asked her when I would be back to see her, even though she knew that I had just left.

She was afraid, and rightfully so.

They didn't want to go to court.

They didn't want to be exposed.

They had to kill my mom quickly.

The next night, Friday, I dreamt that my dad was lying in bed with my mom at the facility, and kissing her forehead. I couldn't see her that day. I wasn't scheduled for a visit. I had a feeling that he would take her soon, but I wanted to be wrong.

I prayed to be wrong.

On Saturday, May 23rd, I found my mom in her bed again. She could barely move. She looked worse than she had four days earlier when I found her in the same bed. She wouldn't even drink her Cuban coffee. I tried to give her small spoons, but she refused. I tried to caress her face and hair, but she pushed my hand to the side, something she had never done before. I crawled into bed with her because that was the only thing that felt right for me. I needed to be close to her.

I held her in my arms.

I closed my eyes and felt the peace and serenity that surrounded my mom.

I left a little early that day also because I knew she needed rest. Clearly, she was not feeling well yet again. I told her that I would be there the next morning. I kissed her goodbye and told her that I loved her, and she said she loved me too. She could barely speak and she was so weak, but her last "I love you" to me will always stay with me. She always knew that I loved her and I knew she loved me.

I woke early the next day, a beautiful Sunday morning. I knew that my visit started at 10 am, but for some reason, I felt that I wanted to get there early. I had this urgency to get there early.

I was worried.

I went to my closet and found one of my dad's work shirts my mom had kept from the late 1960s, early 1970s when my dad worked the grounds at the Miami Springs Golf Course. I had asked her several years earlier if I could take that shirt. I put it on, because I wanted to cheer her up and see her reaction. I felt anxious on the drive. I'm not sure how fast I was going, but I was definitely exceeding the speed limit.

I pulled into the parking lot shortly before 9 am. I gathered the food, coffee, photo album and my purse. The male staff member who met me at the door told me my mom wasn't doing well. I ran in and down the hallway to her room.

He tried to stop me.

A female staff member was standing outside her door. She was crying and also tried to stop me from going inside. I walked past her and into the room. I saw a blond woman on her computer, and then I saw my mom lying in her bed. She looked like she was sleeping.

She was too still to be sleeping, and she didn't look at me when I came into the room.

The hospice nurse who was standing by my mom's bedside typing on her computer, turned to me, very coldly, and said, "you're mom's dead, time of death was 8:55."

My mom knew I was there, she knew.

She died when I drove into the parking lot.

I cannot begin to describe the feelings that overcame me at seeing my mom dead in the small hospital bed, where I had tucked her in and put her to sleep dozens of times. She looked so small lying there.

Her eyes were still open, and she was looking at the picture of her and my dad. Several months earlier, I made her an 8x10 color copy of one of my favorite pictures of my parents. It showed his playfulness, and also his love for her. I had originally placed it close enough to where she could wake up and see it every morning, but someone had moved it farther away. I just moved it back. She had told me that when I put that picture there, she woke up every morning looking at him, and she talked to him every morning. I found comfort in knowing that this picture was the last thing my mom had seen as she went to the next world.

Then all hell broke loose.

I fell to the side of her bed and cried like I had never cried before. I sobbed. I couldn't breathe. I had just lost the most precious and loving gift in my life. I was there for almost 10 minutes before the hospice nurse gave me condolences. She wanted to call and report to the guardian, but I told her that my mom's death ended guardianship. She called her anyway.

Why was I surprised?

These were the people that refused to acknowledge my mom's will and designated health care surrogate.

These were the people that **refused** to speak or meet with me because I wasn't "on the list."

These were the people that had done the guardian's bidding and hit that final nail in the coffin.

I called my oldest daughter and she left work in Gainesville. It was another 45 minutes before she arrived. I had to sit there and wait. In the meantime, I received a call from a social worker from hospice who began to yell at me and insult me. It was about my rights over my mom's dead body. I didn't remember exactly what he said to me, I was angry and hung up the phone.

A couple of my friends and family called me. The guardian did not call or speak to me. Why should she? Her work was done. She faxed a copy of the prepaid funeral package. The package was essentially one hour of visitation at the funeral home, then cremation. No arrangements for a Christian Mass as required by my mom's faith.

I went back to my mom's side. Her body was still warm, her hands were still warm. I couldn't stop crying. I held her hand and put the covers over her. I somehow found that comforting. I wanted to keep her warm, even though her spirit had already left her body.

From her medical records, I read out that she had complained, about 6 am that morning, about having trouble breathing. The staff did nothing to help her. They left her alone, and called Hospice. They left her to suffer and gasp for air. They had been giving her a lethal cocktail. They had forced her die. She had been in pain for weeks, and they did nothing to help her for this either.

I was told by the hospice nurse that morning that she died of **respiratory arrest**, but oddly enough they noted "Parkinson's Disease" as the cause of death on her death certificate. They falsified her death certificate. This did not surprise me either.

At the time this book was being written, one of our most beloved athletic icons passed away, Mohammed Ali. Mohammad Ali had been diagnosed with Parkinson's disease more than 30 years ago. However, according to the media, the cause of his death was NOT Parkinson 's disease, which he had battled for more than three decades, but sepsis, which a bacterial infection in the bloodstream. Most often, a person's death is due to either respiratory failure or cardiac arrest. For example, in my father's case, he died of respiratory arrest due to pleural mesothelioma. It didn't say, "asbestos poisoning."

My daughter finally arrived and we sat there waiting for them to take her body. My daughter and I cried and we held hands. I became angrier. I was there for more than three hours before they came to take her. My sisters never showed up to pay their last respects, but my youngest sister had the time to call and text friends to tell them that my mom had died. Again, I was not suprised one bit.

I gave her one last kiss and then let her go. I felt that the day before had been our goodbye. She was really and truly an angel now. I had to focus on how peaceful and wonderful the place she now was, with my dad, the love of her life, her family and friends who had gone before her. Most important, she was with God. I had no doubt that my mom had gone straight to heaven. My mom had also died in the month of May, which is the month of Mary our Mother. My mom was always very devout to Mary.

I felt numb, sad, destroyed, abandoned, and angry all at the same time. I remember being angry and raging after my daughter got there. I didn't want to see my sisters, but my daughter told me it was their right to see their mother. I didn't think they deserved to see this angel. I was upset because my mom died under guardianship. I had tried so long and hard to free her. My daughter said to me, "mom that part of her life (guardianship) does not define who she was."

She was right, of course. My mom lived a full and amazing life, until guardianship.

I had to talk to people even though I didn't want to talk to anyone. One of my mom's oldest and dearest friends from Cuba, who lived in Miami, called me with her daughters. We had grown up together. We cried together. She adored my mom. She had spoken to my mom on several occasions while in the second lock down on my cell phone.

Many months later, in early 2016, another of my mom's oldest and dearest friends from Cuba, passed away. Her daughter told me that her mother had called out my mom's name a couple days before she died. I told her that my mom was coming to take her. My mom always had that love, that intensity with everyone she cared about.

I vaguely remember thinking that I knew this would happen, and days earlier I had dreamt of my father lying next to her. I just felt like I had more time with her, make more memories, take more selfies, and take more videos of her. I didn't know when she was leaving me, but they knew. The guardianship team plans how and when they will murder their "wards." They needed just enough money to grease the palms of all the players.

It took weeks, maybe even a few months to be able to look at the hundreds of pictures, and dozens of movies, my daughters and I had taken with my mom. We remembered her kindness, her humor, and most importantly her love.

But right now, hours after her death, I felt broken. After four years of fighting for her freedom, and for my right to see my own mother, she had died under guardianship. This happens to thousands of vulnerable elderly who have gone before my mom and were under guardianship. I felt grateful that I was there right at the time of her death, if one is to be grateful for anything. For years, I had nightmares that my mom's body would be taken away after she died without me seeing her for the last time.

I felt I had failed her.

I continued to feel angry for many more months. It was welling up inside me. But there was still so much to do. I still had to make the funeral arrangements. I immediately called our pastor, and picked a date. To my mom, this was the most important thing – to have a proper Catholic service and burial.

My sisters never called to ask if they could help with the funeral arrangements. They never called to ask about my mom. They never spoke to me or my children at the funeral. I never heard them cry once at my mom's funeral.

My children and my son in law were at my side through the whole process, from visiting the funeral home with me to making the final arrangements, to keeping an eye on me, and crying when I cried. They held my hand and we remembered what was important about my mom – she was in heaven now, and she was away from the abuse. She would no longer feel pain, suffering, and misery under an abusive guardian and those who supported them.

From the dozens of stories, emails, websites, and blogs that I had read, guardianship rarely ends on a positive note. The elder – parent, family member, a friend/neighbor – dies under similar circumstances as had my mother. They are isolated, medicated, and their bank accounts drained. Oftentimes, they die alone, with a feeding tube that had been placed to monitor when they would be cut off from nourishment. They also tried to put a feeding tube in my mom, but she refused.[30] The guardian and their attorneys use the "ward's" money to fight the family that is struggling to see them and be with them. The courts, judges and attorneys keep the dysfunction going for years.

I had heard the stories that it continued after the death of the loved one. I was to find out fairly quickly how much ugliness there was yet to experience.

My mom's funeral services were held at St. Patrick's Catholic Church on a beautiful Saturday morning on June 6, 2015. My daughter made all the picture boards that honored her life as a child and young woman in Cuba, as a partner and wife to her soul mate (my dad), and also as a mother and grandmother. My best friend brought flowers. We celebrated the joy in her life after the memorial service. Many of our friends and family were there, some who came from Miami. We cried and honored her.

I found it odd that my older sister's children did not attend the funeral. However, they had been brought to the lock down facility before my mom died to say their "good bye's." There was no remorse or regrets. I heard her laughing at one point during the funeral. I continued to focus on my mom. It was all about my mom.

I was angry at them, and very bitter, but this was my mom's day and no one, including them, could take away who my mom was and what she was about – love. I remember speaking at her memorial, and talking about how much love she had in her heart. I had to sit down because I was shaking inside. I couldn't look at my sisters when I was talking about my mom. I would lose it. I spoke about how much love she had for her brothers and sisters, my dad who was the love of her

---

[30]Feeding tubes are also put in against the elder's wishes when they eat too slowly and/or need assistance. It costs too much at a nursing home to have staff members sit by a patient and lovingly cut food into small bites and let them chew slowly.

life, and her church. My sisters never spoke one word about her at the funeral, not even that she was a great mother.

The day they took her from the lock down facility, I tried to have her body taken to the coroner's office for an autopsy. But the process would entail driving her body up and down I-75 to another city far from Gainesville, because she had died in Ocala. I was emotional, but I made the decision to let that go. Whether it was the right or wrong decision, I cannot say to this day. I didn't need a coroner to tell me the obvious – that my mom had been drugged and slowly murdered for more than three years. All I needed was her medical records to know what they had done, and the time line in which it was accomplished.

CHAPTER 7
Probate and the Estate – We're Taking
Everything Else

About three days after my mom passed, I emailed the former guardian and asked her to please turn over my mom's finances to my attorney. Her response to me was, "now you are sounding like a Baker Act. Best to close your mouth before I sue you."

The Baker Act is Chapter 394, Part 1, Florida Statutes, also known as the Florida Mental Health Act. The Baker Act provides legal procedures for mental health examination and treatment. Criteria for involuntary exam are that the individual: (1) Appears to have a mental illness; (2) Presents a danger to self or others; and (3) Refuses voluntary exam or is unable to understand need for exam. Again, they threatened me with false imprisonment and legal action THREE DAYS AFTER my mom's death.

The former guardian also refused to make a move towards closing the guardianship stating that "this may take from 3 to 6 months." She was wrong.

It was about nine months.

At the writing of this book, it has been more than one year since my mother passed away. I still do not have the letter closing the guardianship from the courts or the judge. This is something that my attorney has not demanded or pursued from the judge.

But, more to come about the clearing out of the estate.

My probate attorney and I filed for the will to be entered as a legal and binding document, for me to be the personal representative and administrator of the estate. All of these requests were granted. The same will that was ignored and denied as a legal and binding document, that was said to not exist, was now an official document.

At the time of her death, my mom still had approximately $26,000 left in one of her bank accounts. They took all of that too, never paid the funeral expenses, and were allowed to take the rest despite not following court procedures and the law.

Welcome to probate court…again.

No final inventory was ever filed in court for my mom's belongings she possessed at the time of her death, at the facility that was operating without a license, the facility that was now in bankruptcy.

The ALF where my mom had been imprisoned for the last 19 months of her life was abandoned and evacuated by September 2015. About two months after my mom passed away, when I was getting all her medical records together, and after finding out that the building had been abandoned, I spoke with the legal representative (trustee) of the man who owned the abandoned lock down facility. He was the one that sent me the medical records. He did not know where my mom's belongings were.

On **February 22, 2016**, the attorney for the guardian (Griffis) filed a fraudulent petition to the court stating that:

- my mom had no tangible property of value remaining,
- at the time of death, the ward owned minimal used clothing and personal effects of no value, no jewelry,
- the daughters of the ward were permitted to take possession of the remaining personal effects of the Ward that they desired….at the direction of Theresa Lyles….and with the consent of the other two daughters.
- remaining furniture was donated or discarded at the direction of Theresa Lyles and with the consent of the Ward's other daughters.

Not only was this not true, but my attorney knew **this was not true.** This never happened, yet a response was never filed even though I requested numerous times that my attorney submit one. No date as to the "alleged" distribution of my mom's belongings was noted in this "official" court document.

Another lie, another smoke screen.

On May 27, 2015, three days after my mom had died, there was a note in my mom's medical record stated "**Guardian to pick up property at a later date.**" This was the last note they put in her medical record.

The funeral package that was purchased for my mom did not include an urn nor did it include the rental of a casket for the church service. I believe this was done on purpose. My oldest daughter and I had to pay for both. According to FS744, these expenses are supposed to come out of the estate during the guardianship. That never happened. I asked two of my attorneys to demand payment from the guardians and from what was left of my mom's estate.

I was ignored.[31]

Almost a week after my mom passed, I wanted to get her belongings. I contacted Memory Lane, and spoke to the manager. She informed me that the (former) guardian (Wolfkill) had instructed her not to allow me access to my mom's belongings until a final inventory

---

[31]It is common for "guardians" to purchase funeral packages that are "subject to cancellation." Before the person dies, the guardian asks for and receives a refund and they pocket the money. There is no audit process for this. The ward is then disposed of at county cost into a pauper's common grave. This process results in more money for attorney's fees, guardian fees and nursing home fees. If the ward has already prepaid for a funeral package which is "subject to cancellation", the "guardian" will cancel it and pocket the money.

had been done. I was informed that if I showed up at the facility, I would not be allowed to enter.

Fortunately, the day my mom passed, I took two things that I knew were dear to her heart – her angel statute and her Virgin Mary medal. I had given her the angel many years earlier after someone had stolen the statute of Mary that she had in front of her home. The day I gave her the angel, she said it was a gift from heaven. When she was taken from her home, I drove by her house one day, before the first guardian cleaned everything out, took the angel, and brought it to the first ALF. It followed her to the second ALF. My mom always wore her medal of the Virgin Mary. She had it for many years. For some odd reason, it was on her dresser that morning she passed. I don't think it was a coincidence.

The statue is in my home, and I've worn the medal since the day my mom died. I never take it off.

I waited until my mom's will was admitted into court as a legal document, and I waited for my letters of administration and personal representation. I also worked on getting all my mom's medical records. Although I suspected and knew what they had done to her, I wanted to see it in writing. I had the right to know now, since they refused to let me know for four years.

I never expected it to be so bad.

People talk about animal abuse and animal shelters and how they feel sorry for the animals and their plight. Don't get me wrong, I love animals, and I am a true animal advocate, but what they did to my mom, how they treated her, drugged her, and withheld medical attention, was my worst nightmare. They tortured her. As I read through hundreds of pages of medical records from the hospitals to the nursing home facilities, and finally hospice, I pictured how my mom dealt with this horror, day in and day out. At one point, I came across a "chemical restraint order" for my mom. I cannot imagine what psychopath would do this to a woman who had absolutely no business being under chemical restraints.

I had read documentation and spoke to people who had lost their family member due to an overdose of drugs in a nursing home. I read how doctors do not even examine the elder, and just give the order over the phone to heavily medicate the person. I imagined my sweet momma being forced to take these drugs that were killing her slowly.

And the most horrifying thing about it was that they were using her own money to kill her.

I had to stop reading many times, because of the anger that I kept feeling inside me. In a way, it may have been a blessing that I didn't know what they were doing to her. I probably would have done something that I would have regretted.

I understand why people get to the point where they feel that murderous anger. I felt it many times. But that was not what my mom was about. She could never hurt anyone. She never complained, and she never said a negative thing about any of these people who murdered her.

When I was able to get my documents in order, and after receiving copies of the medical records, I made the drive out to Ocala to collect my mom's belongings.

As I turned down the road to the facility, I had this incredible sense of foreboding and weird feeling in the pit of my stomach. The parking lot was empty, but the facility van was still parked there. It didn't hit me right away…until I rang the bell, looked inside, and saw that the building had been abandoned.

I panicked.

Thankfully, I called one of my closest and dearest friends and she searched for any information. This is when I found out that the owner of the facility, and another similar facility in Ocala, lived in Georgia. The facility had been operating without a license since September 2014 and had also filed for bankruptcy in early 2015.

I discovered that the guardianship had not provided the courts with an annual accounting for more the two years, since before the second plenary guardian had taken over. The probate judge had issued several warnings to the guardian and her attorney. They were ignored. These warnings should have resulted in imprisonment and/or severe fines. None of this happened.

The guardian and their attorney had been served the letters of authorization and personal representation. They were given a deadline and another warning from the judge. Approximately one week before Christmas 2015, and seven months after my mom had died, the guardian and their attorney finally submitted their report.

The amount they wanted to be paid, just coincidentally, happened to be the exact amount left in my mother's bank account. To the penny...about $26,000.

In their requests were listed dozens of consultations with the first guardian – emails, phone calls and office visits – during the entire time that my mother was under guardianship, and after she her resignation had been official (August 2013). Even though she had resigned and they had closed out her expenses several years before, she was still asking the courts for an additional $27,000, but $12,000 would suffice, because that would leave a "0" balance.

A hearing was finally set on February 22, 2016.

I was being set up.

I had already given my attorneys more than $2500 for "helping" me get through the probate debacle. It was money in their pockets. They knew I would never get this returned out of the estate.

The hearing was in the chambers of a probate judge with me, my attorney, two of the former guardians and their attorney.

I had a bad feeling.

I was not allowed to speak or defend myself during the entire almost 1 ½ hours.

For 45 minutes, I had to hear the first guardian describe what a disruptive person I had been, and why she deserved an additional $12,000. My attorney did not protest or object to most of her slanderous testimony, as I was being bad mouthed and unsubstantiated accusations thrown at me. At one point, and to my surprise, the judge stopped the guardian's tirade. I had to sit there and listen to it yet another time.

The lies and the slander all over again.

They claimed that she was entitled to be <u>a guardian attorney and collect fees</u>, yet my attorney argued that even though it was possible for her to collect fees as guardian attorney, she had never petitioned the court for this privilege. My attorney cited the law (FS 744), and the first guardian admitted several times that she had never filed the correct paperwork. EVER.

Prior to this hearing, I had multiple email exchanges and conversations with my estate attorney, who also worked in the same law firm as the attorney who defended me for most of the time during my mom's guardianship.

Prior to the hearing, I stated that I was not disputing the fees for the last guardian and her attorney. My objections, which I stated multiple times via email, via phone, and in person were with the line items when they consulted with the first guardian. I also vehemently objected to the fees that the first guardian was also trying to collect, more than TWO YEARS after the courts closed her account. In addition, the last guardian and her attorney had never filed a final inventory of my mom's belongings. As I had stated earlier, they filed a fraudulent petition stating that I was present with my sisters at the distribution of my mom's belongings, then donated the remainder to the residents at the facility.

The Friday prior to this last hearing, February 19, 2016, I was contacted by my estate attorney and was told that she would not be at the hearing on February 22nd, and also that the guardian's attorney had contacted her regarding the inventory. My attorney stated that she was told what was eventually filed in court on February 22, 2016.

Again, I didn't have a good feeling that entire weekend, but I tried to stay positive.

After about one hour into the hearing, the judge stopped and stated that he had heard everything he needed to hear, he asked both attorneys to send them their "closing statements" and the hearing was over. I didn't understand what that meant exactly, but felt that everything should be said and decided before we left.

This never happened.

As we were walking out, I spoke with my attorney for the last time. I stated once AGAIN that I did not want the first guardian to receive <u>one cent</u>, which included what she was asking separately and all line items for which the last guardian and her attorney had listed for consultation. I asked him that ALL of these had to be removed.

He stated that it was his opinion that the judge would rule in our favor and not give the first guardian any additional money. Later that day, I emailed him and asked him, once again, to send me his documentation <u>before he sent it to the judge</u>. I wanted to make sure that everything was written as we had discussed on multiple occasions.

He never sent me his response for my review

None of this every happened.

Another smoke screen.

The items that I requested multiple times were never removed from the list of the last guardian and her attorney, and even though she did not abide by the law and admitted to this under oath, the judge awarded the first guardian permission to drain the rest of the money out of my mom's bank account.

No funeral expenses were reimbursed.

Now I know what "take the estate" really means.

They took my mom's life, they took her freedom, they took her home, and they took her money. But there is one thing they could never take, and that was the love and the bond that we had between us, and the love and bond she had with my three daughters.

I have an old jewelry box of my mom's that she had for years. It looks like a treasure chest. When I open it, I can still smell her. I've tried not to open it too often, but when the sadness and pain becomes overwhelming, I open that jewelry box and it soothes me.

Inside are some things that she loved – her mirror, an old scarf, a few pieces of jewelry, and a picture of her and my dad.

My journey began when I was conceived in Cuba. I'm sticking to that story because my mom believed it was so. But my real journey, the one for inner peace began when my mom was placed under the cruelest conditions. She taught me to have so much love and forgiveness in my heart. She healed every part of my body, and left me with one of the most important things about her – love. I'm not sure where this journey of mine will end, but I know that wherever I go, and whatever I do, my mom will be there with me.

I'm trying to be a better mom, friend, and worker. I want to seek and achieve more inner peace, and I know each day my mom's spirit brings me closer to that.

I truly am my mother's daughter. My children say so. When I cry for her some nights, and I call out her name, I can clearly hear her voice in my head saying in Spanish, "don't cry, my daughter. Everything is going to be ok. Pray and leave it in God's hands."

I wrote this book to make people aware and to keep the memory of my mom, my angel, alive. Until my mom was taken into guardianship, I never knew how things really were with elders. This could NEVER happen in my family. We just don't do that to our parents.

This story is about my mom and I – our relationship, our love, and our endless bond. There is a huge disconnect between what I knew my mom to be, and what the medical records and the guardians and my sisters portrayed my mom to be. I have dozens of videos and hundreds of pictures that show her in the light as her close friends and family knew her – coherent, loving, and funny.

But this did happen in my family, after a dispute between my siblings, and we all suffered as a result. The person that suffered the most was my mom.

She was innocent.

She was and still is an angel.

The one hope that I have is that I can save the life of one person from guardianship. If there is a dispute in your family, get counseling or mediation. Do NOT go through the court system because it is a death sentence. The elder rarely gets out alive.

TERESA TOZZO LYLES

Ms. Lyles is an Adjunct Professor since 2014, and a Clinical Research Coordinator at the University of Florida. She was graduated with a PhD in Health Behavior from the University of Florida in 2006; a Masters in Mass Communication from the University of Florida in 1994; and a Bachelor of Science in News Writing and Editing in 1981 from the University of Florida. She has held positions as a Research Coordinator with the Department of Pediatrics at the University of Florida, she has been a Professional Transcriber in several UF Departments and nationwide, and has written a number of scholarly articles in her field and has been a guest lecturer at numerous Paper Presentations.

She has been the recipient of a Graduate Minority Fellowship at the Department of Health Education and Behavior, received a scholarship to the College of Journalism and Communications, and received the Allen, Holyoak and Varnes Scholarship in the College of Health and Human Performance. She is a Certified Health Education Specialist, received a Certificate of Health Communication, is an Advanced Instructor of Adapted Aquatics, American Red Cross ("ARC"), a Teacher of Adapted Aquatics, ARC. Dr. Lyles received a Certificate from the VHA Care Coordination and Home Telehealth ;and a Certificate in Elder Options in Conjunction with Stanford School of Medicine, Leaders Training, and has a certificate from a Phlebotomy Workshop. She is fluent in Spanish. She has three adult daughters and currently lives in rural North Central Florida. You can view her entire CV here: https://drive.google.com/open?id=0B6FbJzwtHocwQjhPNk9JSFlq dHc.

Please note the opinions expressed in this book are strictly those of the authors and are not the opinions of any organization listed in Ms. Tozzo's biography, including the University of Florida or any other institution she has mentioned.

JOANNE M. DENISON

Ms. Denison provided the legal commentary for this book based upon her years of experience in the area of Probate Court Corruption and Court Corruption, in general. She received her Bachelor of Science from the University of Illinois in Chicago in 1979, and her Juris Doctorate (law degree) from Indiana University School of Law in 1985 and was admitted to the Illinois Bar in 1986. After blogging about corruption in the courts since 2009, she was suspended from the practice of Law in Illinois for years by order of the Illinois Supreme Court, despite the fact they knew that the statements on her blog were true; specifically, the Mary G. Sykes probate case 09 P 4585 involved a healthy 90 year old woman who still drove a car, was heavily involved in her local clubs and groups.

In December of 2009, which is the month Mary Sykes was guardianized, Mary G. Sykes played with her local Norwood Park, Chicago, Illinois card group the complicated game of canasta, and according to eye witnesses, as usual, beat the pants off of everyone. She was never served by the Sheriff of Cook County, Illinois, which is required to take jurisdiction. However, that did not stop the judges (Jane Louis Stuart and Maureen Connors) from stripping her of all her assets, throwing her in a series of nursing homes–a place she specified in her advance directives that she did not want to be, and in the end, on May 23, 2015, she was narcotized to death by drugging her with illegal chemical restraints at a nursing home when all the money in her estate ran out. All Mary did was file for an Order of Protection when her eldest daughter, Carolyn Toerpe, took $4,000 from her bank account without authorization. In retaliation, this estranged daughter, Carolyn, filed for Guardianship, and the case was railroaded without any discovery (there is still no discovery on what

Carolyn took from that estate, though we know she drilled out a safety deposit box in her name and the name of Gloria Sykes, without authorization from the court or court order), and emptied it of valuable coins belonging to Mary Sykes having a value of hundreds of thousands of dollars.

At Ms. Denison's trial, one judge would lie on the stand (Jane Louis Stuart) and say that she never chained the other daughter, Gloria Sykes, in her ante room and have her deputies threaten Gloria Sykes with euthanization of her pets if she did not say where Gloria's assets were located so that they could be frozen by the court and then turned over to the Estate to pay the probate attorney's fees. All of the attorneys amassed hundreds of thousands of dollars in fees in a few short years, and if they were not going to be paid by the Estate, then they would use Fraud on the Court to get Gloria Sykes to pay those fees. As a result, a false court order was entered granting over $160,000 in fees to the attorneys, the Estate of Mary Sykes was left fleeced, Mary's home was sold for pennies on the dollar, or unaccounted for, and the 09 P 4585 case, to this day, has not been investigated by the authorities. (The FBI, states attorneys and Inspectors General for the State of Illinois).

In lieu of a proper, honest and thorough investigation, the Illinois Attorney and Disciplinary Commission decided to prosecute Joanne Denison and Kenneth Ditkowsky (another Illinois lawyer who had the audacity to attempt to investigate the Mary G. Sykes case) for making false statements regarding the Mary G. Sykes 09 P 4585 case. Mr. Ditkowsky was told by one of the probate attorneys—Adam Stern, that if Mr. Ditkowsky continued his investigation, Mr. Ditkowsky would be suspended. The ARDC never investigated that threat. Ms. Denison was told by Judge Maureen Connors that if she tried to represent Gloria Sykes, who was a Protective Daughter, Ms. Denison would be disbarred. Both were given lengthy suspensions for trying to protect Mary Sykes from utter destruction of her estate and her murder.

The Sykes Cases remains today, in 2016, uninvestigated by any authorities, after numerous faxes to the authorities, the Chicago Police, the

Naperville Police (where Mary was forced to live with her Plenary Guardian Carolyn Toerpe), the various States Attorneys–Chicago, Cook County and Lisa Madigan, the Illinois Attorney General, as well as the FBI. In addition, it appears that the authorities do not appear to be interested in claiming the taxes due on the false and illegal proceedings where a one million dollar home was sold for pennies on the dollar, hundreds of thousands of dollars in gold and valuable coins went missing, and nearly $200,000 were paid to attorneys in false legal proceedings that had no jurisdiction to issue any orders.

During her long career, Ms. Denison has been associated with the law firms of Cook, Wetzel and Egan; Burditt and Radzius; and, Michael, Best and Friedrich where she was a partner.

Her trademark work includes foreign and domestic prosecution of patents and trademarks, including cancellations and oppositions and appeals before the TTAB and CAFC, and oral arguments and preparation before these courts. Trademark and patent transactional work included extensive foreign and domestic licensing and joint ventures Her patent areas include the fields of basic mechanical, biotech, software and electronics inventions both U.S. and foreign. She has prosecuted litigation appeals to the Illinois Court of Appeals and the Illinois Supreme Court.

She was a member of the Chicago Bar Association. Her activities at the Chicago Bar Association include serving as Chair of the Patents Subcommittee for the years 1987-90, Vice-Chair of the Patent, Trademark and Copyright Committee for the years 1990-91 and Chair of this same committee for the years 1991-92. She also served as legislative liaison for the CBA Women in the Law Committee for 1994-95. Her activities at the Intellectual Property Law Association of Chicago include serving on the Domestic/Foreign Trademark Committee and the Dinner Committee. And, she was for many years on the Chicago Bar Association Special Referral Panel as a recommended Patent, Trademark and Copyright lawyer. She is a former member of the Illinois Bar Association.

She is admitted to practice in the State of Illinois (currently suspended for blogging about corruption in the Cook Count Court

System), the State of North Carolina (inactive and reciprocal discipline), the Court of Appeals for the Seventh Circuit, the Court of Appeals for the Federal Circuit and the U.S. Patent Office (Atty. Reg. No. 34,150).

Ms. Denison is married and has four grown children, Sean, Brendan, Matthew and Melissa.